COMPUTER INTERPRETATION OF
NATURAL LANGUAGE DESCRIPTIONS

ELLIS HORWOOD SERIES IN ARTIFICIAL INTELLIGENCE

Series Editor: Professor John Campbell, University of Exeter

COMPUTER GAME-PLAYING: Theory and Practice
M. A. BRAMER, Thames Polytechnic, London
IMPLEMENTATIONS OF PROLOG
Edited by J. A. CAMPBELL, University of Exeter
PROGRESS IN ARTIFICIAL INTELLIGENCE
Edited by J. A. CAMPBELL, University of Exeter and L. STEELS, Vrije Universiteit, Brussels
MACHINE INTELLIGENCE 8: Machine Representations of Knowledge
Edited by E. W. ELCOCK, University of Western Ontario and D. MICHIE, University of
Edinburgh
IMAGE UNDERSTANDING AND MACHINE VISION
J. GLICKSMAN, Texas Instruments, USA
ARTIFICIAL INTELLIGENCE PROGRAMMING ENVIRONMENTS
Edited by R. HAWLEY, Plymouth Polytechnic
MACHINE INTELLIGENCE 9: Machine Expertise and the Human Interface
Edited by J. E. HAYES, D. MICHIE, University of Edinburgh and L. I. MIKULICH,
Academy of Sciences, USSR
MACHINE INTELLIGENCE 10: Intelligent Systems: Practice and Perspective
Edited by J. E. HAYES, D. MICHIE, University of Edinburgh and Y.-H. PAO, Case Western
Reserve University, Cleveland, Ohio
INTELLIGENT SYSTEMS: The Unprecedented Opportunity
Edited by J. E. HAYES and D. MICHIE, University of Edinburgh
MACHINE TRANSLATION: Past, Present and Future
W. J. HUTCHINS, University of East Anglia
COMPUTER INTERPRETATION OF NATURAL LANGUAGE DESCRIPTIONS
C. MELLISH, University of Sussex
ARTIFICIAL INTELLIGENCE AND SOFTWARE ENGINEERING
D. PARTRIDGE, New Mexico State University
AN INTRODUCTION TO PROLOG
L. SPACEK, University of Essex
AUTOMATIC NATURAL LANGUAGE PARSING
K. SPARCK JONES, University of Cambridge and Y. WILKS, University of Essex
INTRODUCTION TO ARTIFICIAL INTELLIGENCE
M. STEDE
THE MIND AND THE MACHINE: Philosophical Aspects of Artificial Intelligence
Edited by S. TORRANCE, Middlesex Polytechnic
LOGICS FOR ARTIFICIAL INTELLIGENCE
R. TURNER, University of Essex
COMMUNICATING WITH DATABASES IN NATURAL LANGUAGE
M. WALLACE, ICL, Bracknell, Berks
NEW HORIZONS IN EDUCATIONAL COMPUTING
Edited by M. YAZDANI, University of Exeter
ARTIFICIAL INTELLIGENCE: Human Effects
Edited by M. YAZDANI and A. NARAYANAN, University of Exeter

COMPUTER INTERPRETATION OF NATURAL LANGUAGE DESCRIPTIONS

C. S. MELLISH, B.A., Ph.D.
Department of Cognitive Studies
School of Social Sciences
University of Sussex

ELLIS HORWOOD LIMITED
Publishers · Chichester

Halsted Press: a division of
JOHN WILEY & SONS
New York · Chichester · Brisbane · Toronto

First published in 1985 by

ELLIS HORWOOD LIMITED

Market Cross House, Cooper Street, Chichester, West Sussex, PO19 1EB, England

The publisher's colophon is reproduced from James Gillison's drawing of the ancient Market Cross, Chichester.

Distributors:

Australia, New Zealand, South-east Asia:
Jacaranda-Wiley Ltd., Jacaranda Press,
JOHN WILEY & SONS INC.,
G.P.O. Box 859, Brisbane, Queensland 4001, Australia

Canada:
JOHN WILEY & SONS CANADA LIMITED
22 Worcester Road, Rexdale, Ontario, Canada.

Europe, Africa:
JOHN WILEY & SONS LIMITED
Baffins Lane, Chichester, West Sussex, England.

North and South America and the rest of the world:
Halsted Press: a division of
JOHN WILEY & SONS
605 Third Avenue, New York, N.Y. 10158 U.S.A.

© 1985 C.S. Mellish/Ellis Horwood Limited

British Library Cataloguing in Publication Data
Mellish, C. S.
Computer interpretation of natural language descriptions —
(Ellis Horwood series in artificial intelligence)
1. Linguistics — Data processing
I. Title
418   P98
Library of Congress Card No. 85—14660

ISBN 0—85312—828—6 (Ellis Horwood Limited)
ISBN 0—470—20219—X (Halsted Press)

Printed in Great Britain by Unwin Brothers of Woking.

TABLE OF CONTENTS

Foreword 9

1. **Introduction** 11
   1.1 Early Semantic Analysis 12
   1.2 Levels of Noun Phrase Interpretation 15
   1.3 Previous Approaches to Noun Phrase Interpretation ... 17
       1.3.1 Proper Definite Noun Phrases 18
       1.3.2 Pronouns 21
       1.3.3 Indefinite Noun Phrases 22
   1.4 The Basic Problem 26
   1.5 Our Approach 26
   1.6 The Structure of This Book 28
   1.7 A Note on Examples 29

2. **Basic Framework** 30
   2.1 General Context and Choice of Meaning Representation 30
   2.2 The Program 32
   2.3 Example 34
   2.4 Semantic Operations and Interaction with Syntax 34
   2.5 Using the Given/New Distinction 36
   2.6 The Simplest Case 38

3. **Singular Reference Evaluation** 41
   3.1 Reference Evaluation and Early Semantic Analysis 41
   3.2 Constraints and Reference Evaluation 42
   3.3 Representation of Unevaluated References 43
   3.4 Imposing Constraints 45
   3.5 Some More Complex Examples 48
   3.6 Limitations 52
       3.6.1 Other Interfaces to the Database 52
       3.6.2 Incorporating Evidence *for* Candidates 55
   3.7 Relation to Other Uses of Constraints 57
   3.8 Summary 59

4. Indefinite Noun Phrases 60
   4.1 Problems with Coextension 61
   4.2 Problems with Numbers and Quantification 63
   4.3 Dependency Lists 64
   4.4 Semantics of Proposition about Typical Elements 66
      4.4.1 Entities and Sub-entities 67
      4.4.2 Simple Assertions about Typical Elements 69
      4.4.3 More Complex Assertions 70
      4.4.4 Example 71
   4.5 A Note on International Representations 73
   4.6 Limitations—Other Uses of Indefinite Noun Phrases ... 74
   4.7 Summary 74

5. Definite Phrases Referring to Sets 76
   5.1 Representing Definite Sets 76
      5.1.1 Sets with Individuals as Candidate Elements 76
      5.1.2 More Complex Candidate Sets 79
   5.2 Representing 'Each' Phrases 80
   5.3 Summary 83

6. Semantic Preprocessors 84
   6.1 Naming and Linking Dependencies 85
      6.1.1 'External Pairing' 85
      6.1.2 'Each' Quantification 86
      6.1.3 Sharing Information by Linking 89
   6.2 Decomposing Complex Relationships 90
      6.2.1 Unary Operations on Complex Entities 90
      6.2.2 Binary Operations 92
   6.3 Limitations 92
      6.3.1 Restrictions on Communicating Dependencies .. 92
      6.3.2 Problems with Non-distributive Relations 93
   6.4 Summary 95

7. The Inference System 96
   7.1 The Role of the Inference System 96
   7.2 The 'Reference' Rule 97
   7.3 The 'Compound Entity' Rule 99
   7.4 General Proof Strategy 101
   7.5 Problems with Negation 101
   7.6 Summary 102

8. Summary and Examples 103
   8.1 Capabilities of the Program 103
      8.1.1 Reference Evaluation 103
      8.1.2 Operations on Sets 104
      8.1.3 Plural Definite Phrases 105
      8.1.4 'Each' Phrases 105

8.2	Possible Extensions	106
	8.2.1 Complex Constraints on References	106
	8.2.2 Sets of Sets	106
	8.2.3 Questions and Commands	107
	8.2.4 Subsequent Reference to 'Each' Phrases	107
8.3	Major Problems	108
	8.3.1 Other Quantifiers	108
	8.3.2 Complex Statements	108
	8.3.3 Selecting Subsets from Sets	108
	8.3.4 Non-referential Noun Phrases	109

9. Conclusions 110

10. Postscript 113
10.1	Syntactic Parsing	113
10.2	Syntactic/Semantic Scheduling	114
10.3	Semantic Representations	115
10.4	Pragmatics of Language Use	116
10.5	Incremental Semantic Interpretation	116

Appendices 119

1. Constraint Satisfaction Algorithm (See Section 3.4) 121
I.1	Reference Entities	121
I.2	Global Variables	122
I.3	Algorithm to Satisfy a Constraint C	122
I.4	To Filter an Entity r with Respect to Constraints Cs	123

II. Summary of Rules about Dependency Lists 124
II.1	Initial Values of Dependency Lists	124
II.2	Binary Matching Operations on Dependency Lists	125
II.3	Generating 'Corresponding Pairs'	125

III. Meaning of Predicates Used in Examples 127
| III.1 | Main Predicates | 127 |
| III.2 | Predicates Used for 'Semantic Tests' | 128 |

IV. A Note on Functions 129

V. Program Description 131
V.1	Introduction	131
V.2	Basic Strategy	131
V.3	Top Level Control	132
V.4	Syntactic Roles	132
V.5	Constituent Analysis	133
V.6	Semantic Verb Routines	135
V.7	Semantic Preprocessing	136
V.8	Semantic Operations	141

V.9   The Clause Datastructure 143
V.10   Representation of Objects 144
     V.10.1   Indefinite Noun Phrases 144
     V.10.2   Singular Definite Noun Phrases 145
     V.10.3   Plural Definite Noun Phrases 145
     V.10.4   Getting Hold of Dependency Lists 146

VI.   **Program Traces** 147
    VI.1   A Very Simple Example 148
    VI.2   Examples with Definite Reference 150
    VI.3   Operations on Sets 160
    VI.4   Plural Definite Phrases 164
    VI.5   'Each' Phrases 168

VII.   **Bibliography** 176

Acknowledgements

I would like to thank Alan Bundy for his constant encouragement and support in this work. Thanks are also due to Lawrence Byrd, Fernando Pereira, Graeme Ritchie, Mark Steedman, Henry Thompson and Yorick Wilks for their comments on earlier versions of this book.

The work described was made possible by the provision of an SRC Postgraduate Studentship, as well as computer resources associated with SRC grants B/RG 94493 and GR/A 57954.

C. S. Mellish
University of Sussex
1984

FOREWORD

A computer program which can 'understand' natural language texts must have both syntactic knowledge about the language concerned and semantic knowledge of how what is written relates to its internal representation of the world (what it means). It has been a matter of some controversy how these sources of information can best be integrated to translate from an input text to a formal meaning representation. The controversy has concerned largely the question as to what degree of syntactic analysis must be performed before any semantic analysis can take place. An extreme position in this debate is that a syntactic parse tree for a complete sentence must be produced before any investigation of that sentence's meaning is appropriate. This position has been criticised by those who see understanding as a process that takes place gradually as the text is read, rather than in sudden bursts of activity at the ends of sentences. These people advocate a model where semantic analysis can operate on fragments of text before the global syntactic structure is determined—a strategy which we will call *early semantic analysis*.

In this book, we investigate the implications of early semantic analysis for the interpretation of noun phrases. Our initial position will be to regard a noun phrase as providing a *description* of a set of objects in the world, its *referents*. One possible approach is to say that a noun phrase is a self-contained unit and can be fully interpreted by the time it has been read. Thus it can always be determined what objects a noun phrase refers to without consulting much more than the structure of the phrase itself. This approach was taken in part by Winograd [Winograd 72], who saw the constraint that a noun phrase have a referent as a valuable aid in resolving local syntactic ambiguity. Unfortunately, Winograd's work has been criticised by Ritchie, because it is not always possible to determine what a noun phrase refers to purely on the basis of local information. In this book, we will go further than this and claim that, because the meaning of a noun phrase can be affected by so many factors outside the phrase itself, *it makes no sense to talk about 'the referent' as a function of a noun phrase*. Instead, the notion of 'referent' is something defined by global issues of structure and consistency.

Having rejected one approach to the early semantic analysis of noun phrases, we go on to develop an alternative, which we call *incremental evaluation*. The basic idea is that a noun phrase does provide some information about what it refers to. It should be possible to represent this partial information and gradually refine it as relevant implications of the context are followed up. Moreover, the partial information should be available to an inference system, which, amongst other things, can detect the absence of a referent and provide the advantages of Winograd's system. In our system, noun phrase interpretation *does* take place locally, but it does not finish there. Instead, the determination of the meaning of a noun phrase is spread over the subsequent analysis of how it contributes to the meaning of the text as a whole.

Chapter 1

INTRODUCTION

The work described in this book is an attempt to address the question 'How does a natural language text convey meaning and how much of the meaning can a computer program extract as it reads from left to right?' We will concentrate on the interpretation of noun phrases. It is traditional to see a noun phrase as providing a *description* of a set of objects in the world, its *referents*. Thus when we read in a text noun phrases such as:

Mary Smith
the highest mountain in Scotland
a small dog

we normally expect there to be specific objects (some specific girl, mountain or dog) that are being talked about in these phrases. The main aim of interpreting a noun phrase is thus to obtain knowledge of its referents. Of course a computer program may not have direct access to objects in the real world and in this situation we can think informally of the referents as being objects in the machine's internal model of the world. In the case of noun phrases, an attempt to extract too much of the meaning too soon opens the possibility of making incorrect decisions about which objects are referred to. The problems with interpreting noun phrases have led us to formulate a new approach to reference evaluation, which we call *incremental evaluation*. This approach is designed to cope with the claim that

The notion of 'referent' is something shaped by the context of a noun phrase's use, rather than being a simple function of the phrase itself.

The new approach involves three key ideas:

1. The representation and use of levels of meaning *between* the description
   provided by a noun phrase and the set of entities in a world model
   which the phrase is talking about. This includes the representation of
   partially-evaluated references and various kinds of 'typical elements'.
2. The viewing of definite reference evaluation as a *global* problem of
   satisfying consistency constraints and presuppositions, rather than a
   local problem of finding an object satisfying a description. This introduces the possibility of using existing algorithms for constraint satisfaction, such as that used by Waltz [Waltz 72].
3. The idea of expressing the determination of quantifier scope and set
   cardinality by operations on *dependency information*, which represents
   the structure of sets represented by typical elements.

1.1 Early Semantic Analysis

A traditional approach to the computer analysis of natural language inputs
sees the process as being divided into two stages. A first pass ('syntactic
parsing') determines the syntactic structure of the input, expressing it usually in the form of a parse tree. Then a second pass ('semantic interpretation') examines the tree and produces a symbolic 'meaning' on this basis.
For example, a system using this *two-stage approach* might go through the
following stages of representation† for a particular sentence. First of all
comes the sentence itself:

   Two men visited Tom in the bakery.

Then the first pass determines the syntactic structure, which is appropriately represented as a tree:

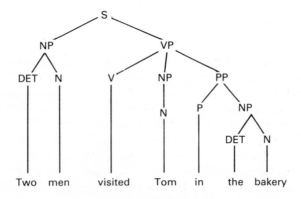

---

† The examples in this chapter are meant to suggest plausible representations for the various
  structures arising in natural language analysis. They are not supposed to correspond to
  anything used by an existing system. The next chapter will discuss the actual representations used in our computer program.

Finally, this tree is 'interpreted' to yield a meaning representation, something like the following, perhaps:

There are two objects 'man1' and 'man2' and a time 't' such that:

man(man1)
man(man2)
before(t,now)
visit(man1,Tom,t)
visit(man2,Tom,t)
location(Tom,t,bakery1)

where 'bakery1' is some already encountered object such that

bakery(bakery1)

Note that, for the stage of semantic interpretation, the syntactic structure of the *whole* of the sentence is available for consultation. Therefore the derivation of meaning can take into account information about the context of phrases as well as information about their internal structure.

This two-stage approach to natural language analysis has been used successfully in practical applications [Woods *et al.*, 72] and is arguably the most straightforward way of obtaining a meaning representation, especially as the first stage (syntactic parsing) is relatively well understood on its own. However, there has been much concern that this rigid separation of syntax and semantics is too inflexible—that the search for efficient, explanatory or psychologically valid models must look elsewhere.

This dissatisfaction is expressed by Riesbeck [Riesbeck 75], who asks why consideration of the meaning of a sentence should have to depend on the successful syntactic analysis of that sentence. He argues that people are not restricted in this way and that there is no reason why computer programs should be. Any alternative to the two-stage approach must involve bringing forward parts of the semantic processing to take place before or during syntactic analysis. It must suggest ways of extracting meaning representations from a sentence before a complete parse tree is available. There will be some degree of emphasis on the incremental accumulation of meaning rather than a sudden burst of semantic activity at, for instance, the end of each sentence. There will also be some amount of emphasis on local semantic processing rather than a global organisation of meaning extraction. Looking at our example sentence, it is clear that bits of meaning can be derived before we get to the end of the sentence. After reading the first two words, we know (more or less) that two men are being introduced into the conversation. So we can start building meaning representations to this effect. After the next word, we know that the men visited somebody at some time in the past, and we can start to represent this information—and so on. All this can happen before any analysis of the sentence as a whole is available.

Let us use the term *early semantic analysis* to refer to the strategy of bringing forward the extraction of meaning in this way. Such a definition is necessarily vague, and we will see in later sections some of the more concrete control regimes that might be covered under this title. Early semantic analysis is concerned with building up the meaning of a piece of text while it is being read and not as part of an appendix to some other process.

What advantages can early semantic analysis give? It could be claimed that researchers *must* consider it if they are ever to develop psychologically real models of language comprehension. However, we will not attempt to consider psychological implications in this book. If we look at the question purely from an engineering viewpoint, we can see possible gains in efficiency. Although it is very hard to make rigorous efficiency arguments in a domain as poorly understood as this, there are plausible reasons why early semantic analysis should be of benefit. Firstly, natural languages are notorious for the ambiguity of their syntax, and frequently the only way to resolve a syntactic ambiguity is to make use of semantic information. If the semantic analysis is proceeding hand-in-hand with the syntactic analysis of a sentence, it can give immediate guidance on any choice that may come up. Early semantic analysis can cut down the syntactic search space by quickly rejecting syntactic structures that make no sense. The alternative is to follow every false path until either a syntactic inconsistency is found or a complete syntactic parse is obtained and then rejected by the subsequent semantic processing. A second argument for the efficiency of early semantic analysis concerns the problem of changing representations. However appropriate parse trees may be as a representation of important sentence structure, they have to be specially built up by syntactic routines and then unpacked again by semantic interpretation in a two-pass system. Early semantic analysis suggests the interpretation of phrases as soon as their structure is apparent and hence the abandonment of unwieldy intermediate representations.

Are there any problems in introducing early semantic analysis? Unfortunately so. Building up the meaning of a sentence incrementally is perfectly straightforward if the sentence is composed of small independent parts. However, as we shall see, it is quite frequent that the interpretation of something early in a sentence depends crucially on the context provided by the rest of the sentence. Early semantic analysis emphasises building up meaning representations locally before the global picture is available, but for many sentences the global structure has a strong influence on the meanings of the individual parts. The presence of these uncertainties imposes limits on the scope of early semantic analysis. The question naturally arises as to what the limits of its usefulness are—just how much early semantic analysis is it feasible to build into a computer program? In this book we will try to answer the question in the context of the interpretation of noun phrases.

1.2   Levels of Noun Phrase Interpretation

What do we mean when we talk about interpreting a noun phrase? We will
start by taking a fairly conventional view of this question. A language-
processing program must be able to assign a 'meaning' to a text as a whole,
in such a way that it can afterwards answer questions and solve problems
related to it. A natural way to organise extracting this 'meaning' is to say
that the individual phrases of the text themselves have meaning, and that
the meaning of a large phrase is a function of the meanings of its sub-
phrases. The meanings of different types of phrases may well be different
types of things. A traditional approach sees a sentence as conveying a
proposition about the world, and a noun phrase as describing some set of
objects in the world. Thus the task of noun phrase interpretation is to
determine what objects in the world a given noun phrase is talking about.
Of course, a computer program will not actually have direct access to these
objects being talked about. Instead, it must relate a noun phrase to some
entities in its *model* of the world.† We call these entities the *referents* of the
phrase. This simple model of noun phrases as talking about specific (sets
of) objects actually does not cover all examples in a watertight way. Nevertheless, for the cases we will consider, it will serve as an adequate starting
point. In particular, we will not have anything to say about 'generic'
reference.

When we come to consider early semantic analysis of noun phrases, we
must actually take into account two kinds of semantic processes:

1. Those that work at the level of noun phrases.
2. Those that work at the level of referents.

The first aspects of a noun phrase that are available for semantic processing come from the words of the phrase and how they fit together. That is,
the first features that are identified are things such as attached determiners,
adjectives and prepositional phrases. As far as these features are concerned, the phrase is a single descriptive unit, irrespective of its semantic
import. Eventually, however, the phrase must be considered as covering a
set of objects in the world and as specifying some properties of these
objects. It is then necessary to consider how many of these objects there
are, whether they are already known about and so on. Semantic processes
acting on the phrase must eventually yield results that say something about
the objects it covers, but there is no reason why some of the processing
should not be based solely on the structure of the phrase itself. Consider a
simple example:

Two particles of mass 5 lbs

---

† In our discussions, we will often blur the distinction between the entities in a world model
and the objects in the world which they are supposed to correspond to, when the context
makes it clear what is meant.

Analysis of this at the noun phrase level can consult the 'meanings' of the words and the syntactic relationships to build up a description like, for instance:

noun_phrase(np23)   measure(np25,5)
determiner(np23,2,indefinite)   units(np25,1b)
isa(np23,particle)
mass(np23,np25)

Such a description can give information about how the referents are to be found ('indefinite', '2') and what properties are mentioned. The properties need not be represented in a way that mirrors the syntactic structure exactly—for instance, one might represent the existence of the adjective 'red' by something like 'colour(np23,red)'. At this level, it is possible to look at the dictionary meanings of words and check on co-occurrence restrictions. For instance, the adjective 'smooth' can only be used with a noun naming a solid object. Also the noun 'table' can mean either a physical table (with four legs, perhaps) or an abstract table (as in a table of numbers). By looking at the alternative dictionary meanings, it is possible to determine the unique sense of 'smooth table'. This is the basic principle behind semantic markers [Katz and Fodor 64].

On the other hand, analysis at the level of referents of the same phrase 'two particles of mass 5 lbs' might decide that two previously unencountered objects are involved, create two tokens for objects ('particle1' and 'particle2', say) and ascribe properties to them (as well as their masses). For example:

isa(particle1,particle)   measure(mass1,5)
mass(particle1,mass1)   units(mass1,1b)

isa(particle2,particle)   measure(mass2,5)
mass(particle2,mass2)   units(mass2,1b)

Because they look very similar in examples such as this, the difference between these two levels of analysis has not been emphasised much in the literature (see, for example, the confusion in [Simmons 73]). Indeed, we have added to the confusion in this example by using the same predicates to mean different things in the two cases. Thus 'isa(np23,particle)' means something like 'the noun of phrase np23 is "particle"' or, perhaps, 'whatever objects np23 refers to are all particles'. On the other hand, 'isa(particle1,particle)' means something like 'the object "particle1" is a particle'. If the kinds of sentences considered only involve proper names or singular indefinite noun phrases (examples such as 'John hit Mary' and 'John has a red ball') then the difference between the levels may be of no practical import. When we use plural phrases or definite reference, however, the difference starts to be significant. For example, a noun phrase level analysis of

The fixed pulley of mass 5 lbs.

would assemble a structure something like:

noun_phrase(np25)   measure(np26,5)
determiner(np25,1,definite)   units(np26,1b)
isa(np25,pulley)
property(np25,fixed)
mass(np25,np26)

but would only be able to assess the reasonableness of the structure by
general considerations (whether pulleys can be fixed and can have masses).
On the other hand, an analysis at the level of referents would be able to use
additional information about particular objects (whether there actually are
any fixed pulleys of mass 5 lbs).

What advantages and disadvantages are there in processing at these two
different levels? In the example of the two particles, much of the processing of the referents was very similar to the noun phrase analysis repeated
twice. This is an unnecessary repetition and would not be practical if the
number of referents was large (or unknown). Processing at this level would
also be a problem if the referents were not ascertainable on the basis of
local analysis (although AI programs tend to assume that they generally
are). Both of these factors limit the usefulness of doing semantic processing
at the level of referents.

Unfortunately, using the noun phrase level also has disadvantages. This
is because even quite superficial semantic analysis cannot always treat
every object covered by a phrase in the same way. There is frequently a
need to consider subsets of objects that behave differently. This would be
the case if the noun phrase was 'two particles of mass 5 and 6 lbs'; we will
consider this problem further in Chapter 6. The necessity for such manoeuvres does not become apparent until one considers operations on sets.
Also, as we saw with 'the fixed pulley of mass 5 lbs', looking at a phrase in
terms of referents can yield stronger acceptability conditions than an
analysis that stops at the phrase level. For it can use information about
what is actually true in the world at hand, as well as what must be true in
every situation.

Finally, most semantic processing at the noun phrase level can actually
be translated into operations at the level of referents. For instance, the fact
that 'smooth' will not go with the abstract sense of 'table' can be seen just
as the fact that it is not possible for there to be a referent which is simultaneously a table of numbers and 'smooth'.

In this book, we will be concerned with how noun phrases relate to a
model of the world, and hence will regard the level of referents as the
primary place to base noun phrase interpretation.

1.3 Previous Approaches to Noun Phrase Interpretation

In this section we will review briefly some of the previous approaches taken
to noun phrase interpretation in computer programs. We will be especially

interested in the extent to which these programs have adopted an 'early semantics' policy, and what problems they have encountered with it.

If the referents of a noun phrase can be obtained as the phrase is read, as we might hope given our commitment to 'early semantics', a possible strategy for a computer program is to determine the referents at the point when it has finished reading the noun phrase. This 'end of noun phrase' strategy for reference evaluation has indeed been used by computer programs, and so let us examine how well it has worked. Consideration of this will reveal some of the problems with early noun phrase interpretation and lead us to develop a more satisfactory formulation.

1.3.1   Proper Definite Noun Phrases

Firstly, what happens in this approach when a definite noun phrase is encountered? For the moment, let us restrict ourselves to considering *proper* definite noun phrases, that is, not pronouns. A definite noun phrase usually provides a description of a set of objects which have already been introduced (Section 2.5). Thus in the 'end of noun phrase' regime, the analysis of a definite noun phrase such as

the blue rod on the green table

will involve no investigation of possible referents until the whole phrase has been read. Then an already encountered object which is simultaneously blue, a rod and on a green table will be selected as the referent.

The idea of performing reference evaluation this early was introduced by Winograd [Winograd 72], who justified it by its utility in resolving certain syntactic ambiguities. For instance, in the sentence

Put the blue pyramid on the block in the box.

there is ambiguity about where the two prepositional phrases should be attached. Two possible readings are shown with bracketing as follows:

Put (the blue pyramid on the block) in the box.
Put the blue pyramid on (the block in the box).

Winograd's point is that the first reading can only be appropriate if there actually *is* a blue pyramid on a block, and the second can only be appropriate if there actually *is* a block in a box. Thus the existence or not of a referent can resolve syntactic ambiguity. In order that it can affect syntactic decisions, it is *essential* that reference evaluation take place at the end of the noun phrase, if not earlier. Unfortunately, Winograd's program suffers as a result from the fact that the referent of a definite noun phrase must be ascertained solely from the information provided by the phrase (and recency considerations).

Novak's program to solve statics problems [Novak 76] follows Winograd's approach closely. However, the program does not use information about the existence of referents to reject inappropriate parses. Instead, it allows for rejection by the use of powerful checks of semantic appropriateness. Thus a locational prepositional phrase will not be attached to a noun phrase if the two underlying objects mentioned are the same. This check serves to reject one possible reading of the following (from [Dull, Metcalfe and Williams 64]):

One painter stands on the scaffold 4.0 ft from one end

Novak's program will not attach the phrase '4.0 ft from one end' to 'the scaffold', because both 'one end' and 'the scaffold' are talking about the same object (the scaffold). Again, the desire to be able to police syntactic decisions with semantic consistency checks motivates the early evaluation of references. This kind of consistency check, using the information in the world model rather than just the information at the phrase level, will be strongly motivated by some of the examples we will consider. Unfortunately, there are two problems with Novak's system. First, the checks are built in as *ad hoc* procedures (he has no proper inference system). Second, the checks are only used to reject *syntactic* possibilities—they cannot influence reference evaluation in any way.

Both of these programs fail to cover an important problem with reference evaluation. When a definite noun phrase occurs in a text, it does not always provide a detailed enough description uniquely to identify the referent. Sometimes even the syntactic and semantic context up to that point do not give much guidance. As a result, it is often impossible to derive the referents of a phrase by the time that phrase has been read. This point was taken up in an important paper by Ritchie [Ritchie 76] criticising Winograd's work. Ritchie showed that the referent of a noun phrase often cannot be determined uniquely on the basis of local processing. For instance, the referent of

the president of the United States

cannot be worked out until one knows the relevant time. So, even with a decision at the end of the noun phrase, it is not possible to guarantee a correct analysis. Instead, it is necessary to take into account how the referent fits in consistently with the context. With 'the president of the United States', the relevant context might be provided by the fact that the discourse is discussing the state of the 'arms race' in 1962. On the other hand, it might be provided by a time adjunct such as 'in 1962' that does not appear until later in the sentence. Examples such as this seem to provide a strong argument against the 'end of noun phrase' approach. One might propose some other unit apart from the noun phrase to determine the occurrence of reference evaluation. For instance, it might be possible to evaluate all references at the end of the sentence, or perhaps at the end of the paragraph. However, it seems likely that one could extend Ritchie's argument to show that no arbitrary unit can guarantee the presence of enough information for reference evaluation in every case. What is needed is a much more flexible mechanism, and this is what our system of *incremental* evaluation will provide.

Let us consider a more complicated example where the global context is important—a description of a complex physical configuration. The following example is from [Loney 39]:

A hollow vertical cylinder, of radius 2a
and height 3a, rests on a horizontal
table, and a uniform rod is placed
within it with its lower end resting on
the circumference of the base . . .   (1.1)

Here there are two pronouns and a definite noun phrase to resolve (these are shown underlined). The local semantic context can provide some useful information—for instance, because of the meaning of 'within', the first 'it' must be a reference to the hollow cylinder (the only hollow object available). However, both the cylinder and the rod have ends, and so we cannot initially tell what 'its' refers to. Also, 'the base' could conceivably refer to part of the cylinder or part of the rod (or part of the table?). So the other two references are not at all straightforward. In order to resolve these, we must bear in mind the global situation and what physical configurations are possible. That is, we must look *outside* the noun phrases to see what else is being said about the referents and whether it fits in with what we already know. For instance, an end of the rod cannot rest on part of itself. Also, the rod being inside the cylinder precludes part of the cylinder resting on part of the rod. These restrictions mean that in fact some of the possible interpretations can be quickly ruled out.

Ritchie's analysis and our example demonstrate how important it is to take into account global conditions of consistency. It is impossible to do this if an arbitrary decision is made about when references are to be evaluated. However, the only reliable alternative seems to be to postpone reference evaluation indefinitely. This would be in direct violation of our goal to pursue early semantic analysis.

Yet another problem with this 'end of noun phrase' mode of reference evaluation from an 'early semantics' point of view is that noun phrases can be complex and may even contain relative clauses, as in

The string which hangs over the fixed pulley at an angle of a1.

If we are not allowed to consider referents of the head noun phrase until an analysis has been made of the whole relative clause, the aim of 'early semantic analysis' is hardly being fulfilled, for an arbitrary number of words may have to be read before we come to work out the noun phrase referent. Also, the amount of semantic analysis that can be carried out on the embedded clause in the first pass is severely restricted by the fact that the referent of one of the most important noun phrases is not available. So we can criticise this mode of reference evaluation both for its inability to allow for contextual factors and for its failure to keep to the spirit of early semantic analysis!

In summary, then, we have seen two problems with the approach of obtaining definite noun phrase referents after the phrase has been read:

1. Because of the importance of the global 'environment' of the phrase, this may not be late enough to make a sensible choice.
2. Because noun phrases may be complex structures, considering referents at this time may be too late for any kind of early semantic analysis of embedded clauses.

How have other workers dealt with the problems of definite noun phrases? The only other approach has been to postpone reference evaluation until a first pass of the input is finished. Those systems employing the two-stage model of natural language analysis have adopted this approach, which has been very successful in practice. However, we clearly cannot build on this in constructing an approach to early semantic analysis. The two-stage approach has been used by Woods [Woods *et al.*, 72] in his system for answering queries about lunar rock samples. In addition, Schank's SAM system has much of this flavour. For, although the first pass of the system (the operation of the ELI parser) is building semantic structures, the analysis is only at the noun phrase level at this stage, and reference evaluation is performed by a separate module (MEMTOK) operating afterwards. Charniak's program to understand children's stories [Charniak 72] does not operate with natural language inputs at all, but works entirely on formulae of a meaning representation language. Hence there can be no question of reference evaluation occurring before the overall structure of the meaning is apparent. Brown and Burton's SOPHIE program also postpones the evaluation of complex noun phrases. Thus the result of local analysis of 'the voltage at the collector of Q5' is a *program* to be run when the student's question is answered—represented in their notation by (MEASURE VOLTAGE (COLLECTOR Q5)).

In conclusion, none of the existing systems provides the combination of an early derivation of referents with the sensitivity to context that Ritchie shows to be necessary. Given this unfortunate state of affairs, the only way forward is to devise a completely new approach to reference evaluation. We have seen how the determination of a noun phrase's referent can require the consideration of any amount of the context of that phrase. Our approach will be to see this fact from another angle. We will say that a 'referent' is something provided by the context, with only some help from the noun phrase itself. Hence it makes no sense to centre the whole interpretation around the noun phrase. Early semantic analysis *is* still possible, but it is necessary to be more flexible about when reference evaluation happens. Instead of seeing it as a process with a fixed start and end, we must view it as a continuing, *incremental* process.

1.3.2 Pronouns

Let us now consider pronoun referents. Here, the noun phrase itself does not provide much information about the referent, and some contextual information must be used. A common technique is to have available a 'history list' of objects that have been mentioned in the discourse. This provides a set of candidate referents, and a choice can be made on recency and other criteria. The programs of Charniak and Schank contain interesting mechanisms for resolving pronoun references by seeing how the proposition expressed manifests something that was already 'expected' to ocur in a given context. However, as we have noted, neither of these programs has anything to say about how one can begin to evaluate references as one reads from left to right.

The programs of Winograd, of Novak and of Brown and Burton all use the 'history list' idea. Winograd [Winograd 72] postpones the derivation of pronoun referents until the end of the sentence, at which point a decision is made, on the basis of syntactic clues. Novak uses recency as well as person/number agreement to pick a referent. Brown and Burton's system is more refined, because their semantic grammar can actually predict what kind of object a pronoun referent or deleted object must be. This cuts down the set of objects on the history list that need to be considered. However, the restrictions that can be expressed are only ones of simple class membership. Other kinds of consistency checks are not possible. Finally, the work of Grosz [Grosz 77] suggests that the notion of history list can actually be refined to take more account of the structure of the discourse.

As we saw in the last section, evaluating references can require information about the consistency of the meaning as a whole, as well as information derived from the phrases themselves. This is particularly important with pronouns, which in themselves give little information about what they refer to. However, none of the existing systems combines an 'early' approach to pronoun interpretation with the possibility of having consistency checks of any power.

1.3.3   Indefinite Noun Phrases

The majority of AI natural language processing programs have been designed around the idea of answering questions about and carrying out operations on a given database. The programs of Woods [Woods *et al.*, 72], Winograd [Winograd 72], and Brown and Burton [Brown and Burton 75] all fall into this category. In such situations, it is not a significant task for the program to accept declarative information about the world it operates on. As a result, few programs (Novak's [Novak 76] being an important exception) have attempted to deal with declarative information in any significant way. In this book, we will be concerned almost entirely with declarative sentences. This immediately leads to some differences.

Perhaps the main difference between the two approaches is in the treatment of indefinite noun phrases. In questions and commands, such phrases represent 'patterns' or combinations of properties that will become descriptions of goals for a theorem prover or problem solver. For instance, in Winograd's program, the noun phrase 'a red cube' in the context of

Is there a red cube behind a pyramid?

gives rise to the following PLANNER description, which is a program for finding such an object:

```
(THPROG (X1)
    (THGOAL (#IS S?X1 #BLOCK))
    (#EQDIM S?X1)
    (THGOAL (#COLOUR S?X1 #RED)))
```

Since the existence of such an object is only questioned and not asserted, it is not appropriate for understanding the sentence to consider how reasonable this description is or how many objects it could cover. The idea of the phrase having a 'referent' seems to make no sense. On the other hand, in a declarative sentence an indefinite noun phrase can often be seen as having a referent, and it is possible to set up appropriate entities in the world model. This is what happened in our example representation of 'two men visited Tom in the bakery'. Here it is possible to build up a 'concrete model' of what the sentence is saying and how it relates to the world as it is read. We will present here only mechanisms for dealing with declarative sentences. A preliminary idea for extending our approach to questions and commands is mentioned in Section 8.2.3.

While looking at indefinite noun phrases, we should consider how Novak's program treated them. As with definite noun phrases, Novak always took the approach of finding referents as the phrases were read. The assumption was that an indefinite noun phrase was used to introduce some number of previously unencountered objects. In order to determine the number of objects, various heuristics were used. One heuristic was to assume the number 2 for an unnumbered phrase that was plural but not compound. Another was to take the number from the number of locations if a location modifier was present. Hence Novak could determine that there are two piers in the following (from [Dull, Metcalfe and Williams 64]):

A bridge 60 ft long is supported by a pier at each end.

because of the existence of the location modifier 'at each end'. Of course, this heuristic will not work except sometimes when an 'each' phrase is used to describe the locations. Thus in the sentence:

There is a man beside the two urns.

there need only be one man. Finally, the program sometimes had to resort to creating additional referents if the initial guess turned out not to work. Thus in his analysis of the following (from [Dull, Metcalfe and Williams 64]):

A painter . . . stands on a plank . . . which is supported at each end by a stepladder the semantics of 'support' require a separate support for each end and hence create an extra referent in addition to the one already created for 'a stepladder'. Such a revision of a previous piece of semantic analysis (the evaluation of this indefinite noun phrase) deserves a more principled treatment than Novak provides. How is it guaranteed that meaning structures already built on the basis of there being a single stepladder will still be valid when the number of objects is changed?

Novak's heuristic rules work for the examples he gives, but do not tackle the problem of indefinite noun phrases with any generality. We will attempt to deal with the following two problems in a more principled way.

1. The problem that many first references to sets are made in such a vague way that local analysis cannot sensibly make decisions about cardinality. In the following (from [Richards *et al.*, 66]):

> Small blocks, each of mass m,
> are clamped at the ends and
> at the centre of a light rod.   (1.2)

the normal interpretation is that there are three blocks, one on each end of the rod and one in the centre of the rod. However, in a left-to-right analysis of the sentence, the number of blocks is not known until a relatively late stage (when a pairing between blocks and positions on the rod is made). It is impossible to carry out semantic analysis reliably in terms of individual blocks until that stage is reached. Moreover, it would be foolish to try to guess the number of objects early in order to resolve the uncertainty.

2. The problems introduced by the possible presence of quantification. Note that we will only consider here quantification over finite, known sets. The following example is from [McKenzie 60]:

> A wooden stool 2 ft 2 in high consists of . . .
> a uniform vertical leg at each corner.   (1.3)

In this sentence, the initial 'leg' noun phrase seems to refer to a single object until the quantifier is discovered later on in the sentence. What was a single entity now has to be considered a 'prototypical member' of a set of (three?) legs. It is inappropriate for semantic analysis to make too many early decisions in such cases.

We might ask whether any of the existing work on quantification provides any help with these problems of early semantic interpretation. Indeed, computer programs which can interpret complex combinations of quantifiers have been developed, following the ideas of Woods [Woods 77] and Colmerauer [Colmerauer 77]. It is important to note, however, that the aim of Woods and Colmerauer was to provide rules for translating from quantification in English to quantification in a logical formalism, taking into account all the information available. It was not part of their aim to see how sentences with quantification could be understood in an early semantics framework. In this respect, their work differs fundamentally from ours. There is no reason to expect that approaches with such different aims need have anything much in common. Indeed, Woods' and Colmerauer's work has not proved suitable for use in a system using early semantic analysis. Conversely, our own work has not suggested any new rules for determining quantifier scopes or even proved to cover examples of the complexity dealt with by these two-stage systems.

The main thing to note about the approaches of Woods and Colmerauer is that they both involve building up a structured logical formula for the meaning of a sentence. Thus, for instance, Colmerauer's representation of the sentence:

The man gives a ball to each child.

would be something like:

```
the(x1,man(x1),
   each(x2,child(x2),
       a(x3,ball(x3),
          gives(x1,x2,x3)
         )
        )
     )
```

The trouble with using this kind of representation is that it means that the meaning cannot be accumulated incrementally—each part of the structure can only be interpreted given its place in the whole. In the example, the interpretation of 'a ball' is buried in the structure and not a separable item about which inferences can be made. The advantage of considering the logical structure of a sentence as a whole is that rules about quantification scope can take into account the global position. Thus it is possible to formulate rules such as:

> The quantification introduced by the article of the subject of a verb dominates the quantifications introduced by the complements closely related to that verb.

(from [Colmerauer 77]). It may be that this approach is the most general way of tackling complex interactions between quantifiers, but it remains to be shown that it can make any contribution in a system carrying out early semantic analysis. Indeed, our approach will be quite different, and we will deal with simple quantification by performing local operations on sets (Chapter 6).

In conclusion, indefinite noun phrases covering sets of objects provide another example of where the 'referents' of a noun phrase can only be determined by a consideration of the context. Existing programs cannot provide much guidance here. Our model of incremental noun phrase interpretation will cope with this.

1.4   The Basic Problem

The basic problem with the early semantic analysis of noun phrases is that full information about referents is not always available before the context is taken into account. Moreover, the relevant context may not be provided until some time after the original noun phrase is read. Therefore any attempt at an early derivation of referents will be faced with serious uncertainties. We have seen examples of this in two main areas:

1. In the interpretation of definite noun phrases and pronouns, where criteria of global consistency may be essential to narrow down the possible referents.
2. In the interpretation of indefinite noun phrases, where cardinality information cannot always be determined before later noun phrases have been read.

Existing work that attempts to derive referents at the time a noun phrase is read suffers from both of these problems. However, the only alternative seems to be to abandon early semantic analysis altogether. We will show that this is not necessary—that, given a suitable representation system, it is possible to carry out a significant amount of early semantic processing without suffering from these particular problems of uncertainty.

1.5   Our Approach

If early semantic analysis leads to serious uncertainties in certain situations, one solution is to simply abandon it in those places. We can then describe its limitations by characterising when the problems arise. However, such a solution would do little to reveal the underlying reasons for the problem. An alternative approach is to look more closely at the kind of semantic analysis we are considering and see why it is letting us down. Problems with uncertainty often indicate an inadequate representation of a problem domain, and it is possible that while trying to represent inappropriate factors we are missing out on important information. That is, if we could represent what is conveyed by the text rather than what we would like to be there, the problems might disappear. The basic idea of representing and reasoning about the incomplete information provided by an input, rather than trying to force a decision about its overall significance, has already been used by Marcus [Marcus 79] for syntactic analysis, Bobrow and Webber [Bobrow and Webber 80] for the semantic interpretation of verbs, and Brady [Brady and Wielinga 77] for computer vision. Brady argues that a vision program should explicitly represent partially-formed percepts and should operate by incrementally refining these. At each stage, it should be guided by the information that can be computed most cheaply.

The fundamental assumption that we will challenge here is that referents are things that belong essentially to noun phrases. Instead, we will see them as being determined by global consistency conditions, only some of which are contributed by noun phrases. Following up this idea, we develop a system of representation for the interpretation of noun phrases. Using this, it is possible to express the various kinds of partial information that noun phrases actually provide. Moreover, most processes of inference and semantic interpretation can carry on working with this representation system because they simply do not need anything more specific. Because irrelevant decisions are not forced, it is actually possible to introduce much more early semantic interpretation than the above discussion might suggest.

Before looking in detail at the representation system, let us briefly review some of the characteristics it must have. Ideally we should be able to make use of precisely the information that is given unambiguously by the text, gradually refining this to accommodate more information as it arrives. Semantic analysis should be as thorough as it can without having to make ill-advised decisions, so that it can provide a good check on syntactic choices but so that backtracking is never necessary. Thus ideally it should be possible to:

— store results of semantic processing without overcommitment with respect to questions that cannot be decided;
— accumulate disambiguating information smoothly so that it is not necessary to redo or undo previous work;
— use what information is available in inferential processes to implement consistency checks of reasonable complexity.

In summary, the representation should allow us to build up noun phrase meanings *incrementally* as the relevant information arrives, rather than according to some strict timing principle.

The way that we introduce the new representational ideas involves enriching the usual notion of 'world model'. There is no reason why the entities represented in a world model need correspond in a simple way to the objects in the world. It suffices only that the symbols and what they represent provide a consistent view of the world that supports whatever language task is being undertaken. We introduce the idea of having symbols in the world model to represent a variety of different kinds of *underspecified* and *intensional* objects. Having these extra objects available makes it possible to represent certain kinds of vague statements—by expressing them in terms of suitable symbols in the world model. Because of the intensional nature of some of the objects, information about a single world object may be expressed in the model in terms of several different symbols. Thus the system must constantly keep track of how different objects in the model relate to one another in the world and how partial specifications are gradually enriched. Specifications become enriched partly through the operation of *reference evaluation as a constraint satisfaction process* and partly through the communication of *dependency information* about cardinality and scope. The extra information kept about the entities in the model provides an important input to an inference system designed to reason about what is actually true in the world.

If we wish to develop a representation system of this kind, it is necessary not only to consider the semantics of what is represented but also to ensure that appropriate algorithms exist to make use of the representations. Hence we will be considering to some extent how the system of representation can actually be used to carry out early semantic analysis. The discussion will focus on the performance of a running computer program (described more fully in Chapter 2 and Appendix V) that 'understands' mechanics problems stated in English.

1.6   The Structure of This Book

The main structure of this book reflects the gradual building up of a system of representation for *incremental* noun phrase interpretation. The development begins with an extremely simple system and ends up with a scheme which is complex enough to confront most of the problems we have discussed. At each stage it is considered how the representation can actually be used in a natural-language-understanding system. This is illustrated by examples from the computer program.

Chapter 2 gives an outline of the starting point of the work. It describes some basic assumptions and the framework on which our program has been built. In particular, it shows how noun phrases can be dealt with in the simplest possible case—where each phrase introduces a single new object.

Chapter 3 discusses how singular definite reference can be incorporated into such a system. It is suggested that reference evaluation should be seen as a classical *constraint satisfaction* task, so that filtering algorithms such as that of Waltz [Waltz 72] can be used. This enables semantic interpretation to retain its incremental character. It also introduces special 'reference entities' into the world model.

Chapter 4 develops a more sophisticated representation for the interpretation of indefinite noun phrases. The intensional significance of world model entities is emphasised and the status of reference entities seen in a more general framework. The notion of *dependency lists* is introduced, to represent partial information about sets and quantifier scope.

Chapter 5 looks at some other phrases that refer to sets. The representation of plural definite references and 'each' phrases is developed, with the existing mechanisms for definite reference being appropriately extended.

Chapter 6 investigates further how propositions about sets can be analysed and how the dependency list representation can be used in this. In particular, it shows how matching operations on dependency lists allow information about set cardinality and quantifier scope to propagate.

Chapter 7 goes into some more detail about the inference system needed to support consistency checks using the representation developed.

Chapter 8 gives a set of examples to characterise the scope of our methods and some of the remaining problems. This is followed by some conclusions about what has been discovered about the possibilities for early semantic analysis.

1.7 A Note on Examples

Before the main part of this book begins, it is appropriate to make some remarks about the examples that appear throughout the text. Examples whose sources are cited are quoted as they appear in the original sources; all other examples have been constructed by the author to illustrate specific points. It should not be assumed, unless it is explicitly stated, that an example appearing in the text can be processed by the computer program.

Chapter 2

BASIC FRAMEWORK

This chapter describes the basic framework on which our computer program is built. The theoretical ideas of the book are meant to stand on their own, independent of their use in a particular program. Nevertheless, the discussion is made more concrete if we can give examples using a specific program. Also, because the ideas are obviously intended to be incorporated in a computer program, it makes sense to indicate how they fit into at least one natural-language-understanding program as a whole. Therefore we will say a few words about our program as such. Some of the description of the domain of application (mechanics problems) and the kind of syntactic analysis undertaken is only relevant to this program. Other parts of the description, relating to the basic structure model and the use of the given/new distinction, must apply to a large extent to *any* program that is to make use of the theoretical ideas.

2.1 General Context and Choice of Meaning Representation

The work described here has taken place in association with a wider research project [Bundy *et al.*, 79] to develop a computer program that can solve mechanics problems stated in English. Working in such an environment inevitably means that certain common assumptions must be held, standards of compatibility must be adhered to and that attention is focused mainly on problems in the restricted domain under consideration. This section introduces some of the conventions that underlie the work and characterises the limitations involved in considering only mechanics problems.

We use the notation of Predicate Calculus throughout to represent pieces of 'meaning' and pieces of the world model that a computer program might build up. Thus relationships are represented as predicates and objects in the world as logical terms that can appear as arguments to the predicates. This decision is not vital to the work described—it could be implemented in a very similar way using a Semantic Net formalism. Indeed, there are well known methods of translating between the two formalisms. A definition of some of the main predicates that we use in examples is given in Appendix III.

An important assumption behind the ideas presented here is that in general the semantic analysis necessary for 'understanding' a sentence must involve complex mechanisms that need to call on the full power of an inference system. This is strongly motivated by the study of mechanics problems, for the kinds of representations that will allow a problem-solving program to perform such intricate manoeuvres as resolving forces and calculating relative velocities must necessarily be detailed and specific. Hence the semantic analysis must elucidate many details of the physical configuration that are not directly available from the text. The choice of predicates in the representation needs to enable subtle distinctions and fragments of information to be expressed, and so a relatively simple predication in English may expand into a number of basic assertions. Although the examples given here will not emphasise this aspect, the fact that semantic analysis must have this depth has been an important consideration.

What are the important features of mechanics problems that distinguish them from other uses of language? A mechanics problem can be viewed as the presentation of a tiny world which is completely isolated and self-contained and about which some interesting features are to be derived. No prior knowledge of the particular situation is required on the part of the reader, who must use his general knowledge together with the problem statement to produce an accurate model of all the important aspects of the world presented. A consequence of this is that the main emphasis is on processing declarative information, assimilating new knowledge into a growing world model rather than answering questions about information known in advance. The mechanisms presented here are primarily designed for declarative sentences, although extensions to cover questions and commands are considered in Section 8.2.3. A second consequence is that the kinds of information conveyed are normally restricted by the finiteness of the worlds described. There are usually a finite number of objects and a finite (if large) number of possible relationships (this may not be the case in some representations of continuously-changing systems). As a result, quantification tends to be over finite sets and the use of complex logical connectives is not very common. The 'meaning' of the problems we consider can always be expressed as a simple conjunction of atomic propositions (unit assertions) containing no variables. We have made full use of this in designing ways of handling information. The restrictions on quantification have also been an important factor, and it is not clear whether the mechanisms described can be extended to handle quantification in general.

Finally, the domain of discourse in mechanics problems is restricted. Mechanics problems do not talk about intentions or human interactions, for instance. Instead, the emphasis is on simple physical relationships, such as contact and support, and changes of state, such as movement and collision. How relevant this restriction is to the kinds of semantic processes that are involved is not clear.

2.2   The Program

The ideas that are presented here have been explored in the development of a computer program to work in the mechanics domain. This program takes as input English statements of mechanics problems and produces meaning representations suitable to be used by the mechanics problem-solving program. It makes use of domain-specific semantic routines written by Martha Palmer. This book will not discuss the semantics of mechanics problems, and we will give examples were the semantic processing has been greatly over-simplified, for we are more concerned with how the semantic routines fit into the overall structure than with what their internal properties are. The framework that is developed is intended to be as independent as possible of the subject matter, and so a detailed discussion of the semantics would be out of place here.

The structural model on which the program is built is shown in Fig. 2.1. The idea is that the top level of control is some sort of syntactic analysis, which calls semantic routines (semantic operations) as early as possible (see Section 2.4). In the more complex cases, a stage of preprocessing is necessary (this is explained in Chapter 6), but this can be ignored for now. Semantic operations generate assertions, which represent constraints to be satisfied or new information to be recorded in the database (Section 2.5). The satisfaction of constraints in turn requires the use of an inference system (Chapter 7). This takes into account the known inference rules, extra information about the objects in the world model and the information in the database. The types of extra information about objects that we use will become clear as the representational system is developed.

The program is written in Prolog [Clocksin and Mellish 81], a programming language based on Predicate Calculus. Prolog provides an automatic backtracking facility, but the program has been carefully designed to avoid unconstrained backtracking as much as possible. Nevertheless, in certain situations (as will become clear) it is necessary to rely on backtracking as a last resort, and so it is arranged that every action (including adding something to the database) can be undone if necessary. Some traces generated by the program are given in Appendix VI, and more details about the implementation are to be found in Appendix V.

The program's top level syntactic analysis is expressed as a Definite Clause Grammar [Pereira and Warren 80] and behaves in much the same

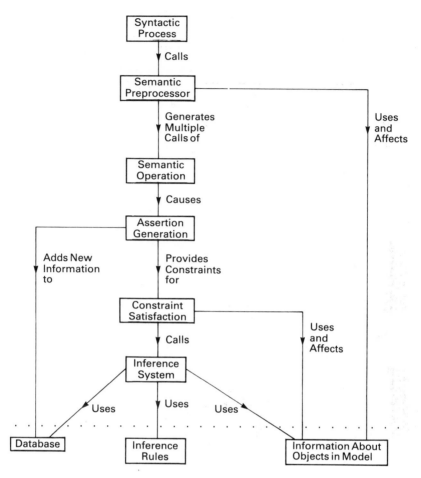

Fig. 2.1 – Basic structure of the program

way as a traditional ATN parser with mixed top-down and bottom-up processing. At the clause level, it tries to collect up a set of top level constituents (noun phrases, prepositional phrases, verb groups and so on), interpreting each one semantically as it finds it. Then, finally, a semantic routine associated with the main verb is invoked to interpret the main preposition being expressed. The treatment of noun phrases involves first moving to the head noun, using this to obtain a 'referent', then interpreting each adjectival phrase before the noun. Finally, each modifier after the noun (prepositional phrase, relative clause, etc.) is interpreted semantically as it is syntactically parsed. No syntax trees are built up during noun phrase analysis. Relative clauses are treated as ordinary clauses where the referent of the head noun phrase fills some syntactic role (subject, object of a preposition, etc.).

It can be seen from this brief description that the program falls short of the ultimate application of early semantic analysis in many ways. The main limitations are the postponement of the verb semantics and the delayed treatment of pre-nominal adjectives. The work of Bobrow and Webber [Bobrow and Webber 80] suggests an approach to the incremental analysis of verbs (although their system works at the level of phrases rather than referents). It would be interesting to see how such a system could be combined with ours, although this would be largely irrelevant to the problems we are immediately concerned with. In order to study the problems of early noun phrase interpretation that we have mentioned, it suffices to have a system that interprets noun phrases as they are read. In this respect, our program performs adequately enough to be a useful research tool.

2.3   Example

Figure 2.2 shows the input and output of the program for part of a simple mechanics problem. The meanings of the predicates used are given in Appendix III.

A particle of mass b rests on the smooth table.

    isa(particle,particle1).
    mass(particle1,mass1,period1).
    measure(mass1,b,arbs).
    point_of(table1,point1).
    contact(particle1,point1,period1).

Fig. 2.2 – Sample input and output.

It is assumed here that a smooth table has been mentioned in some previous input, and that the symbol 'table1' has already been assigned to represent it in the world model. The symbols 'particle1' and 'mass1' are new symbols that are created in response to this sentence—standing for the particle and its mass respectively. 'period1' represents the period of time over which these relationships are supposed to hold. As a result of this input, five new assertions are added to the database. Various other assertions, which serve to identify the referent 'table1' by saying that it is smooth and a table, are considered by the program, but must be in the database before this sentence is processed.

2.4   Semantic Operations and Interaction with Syntax

Although we see early semantic analysis as an important factor of a natural-language-understanding system, we do not reject syntactic analysis as an unimportant part of the language processing. Indeed, it is hard to see

how any semantic analysis of the text can take place before some preliminary syntactic processing (such as recognising simple groupings of words
and taking account of basic word order) has occurred. The position of
considering a stage of syntactic analysis does not contradict the overall goal
of introducing early semantic analysis. Instead, it means that semantic
processes must be closely anchored to syntactic ones, so that as soon as a
fragment has received some syntactic classification it can be semantically
interpreted. In the work of Winograd [Winograd 72], the semantic analysis
is divided between a small set of 'semantic specialists'. Thus, for instance,
there are two specialists associated with noun phrases, and the semantic
processing of a whole noun phrase is distributed between just the two of
them. We follow Ritchie [Ritchie 77] in believing that it is productive to
decompose these specialists into smaller routines. By making the 'grain' of
the semantic processing smaller we can invoke semantic routines earlier
and can generally increase the amount of interaction with syntactic
analysis.

The result of this decomposition in our program is a set of *semantic
operations* which act on small syntactic and semantic fragments. Typically,
a semantic operation will be associated with a particular syntactic category
or sub-category. Thus in the computer program there is an operation to
apply an adjective to a referent, find a dimension (for instance, height,
weight or velocity) of a referent, interpret a preposition relating two referents and so on. The action of a semantic operation in general involves
expanding out the meaning of a word (adjective, dimension, etc.) applied
to a referent or referents into assertions about them. It follows from the
kinds of words mentioned that the operations are mainly binary and unary.
Not all semantic operations are tied to specific syntactic items—for
instance, in the mechanics world a fundamental operation is predicating

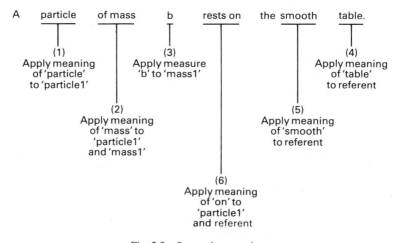

Fig. 2.3 – Semantic operations.

contact between two objects. However, this can be expressed linguistically in many ways and instances of contact may only be implicit in descriptions of other relationships. The semantic analysis of verbs tends to involve a decomposition into more primitive operations such as this (see [Palmer 81]).

Figure 2.3 indicates the semantic operations that would be invoked in the simple example. They are numbered to reflect the order in which the program would invoke them.

(We have been deliberately vague here about what kind of referent the meanings of 'table' and 'smooth' are applied to. The whole point about these semantic operations is that they serve to *identify* the referent in this example. Exactly what form the referent takes before it has been fully determined will be investigated in Chapter 3.)

2.5 Using the Given/New Distinction

The purpose of semantic analysis in our program is to create tokens for objects known to exist and output a set of assertions in terms of these to express information about the world. As the natural language analysis proceeds, more and more output assertions are produced. At each stage the system has a partial model of the world, and the assertions generated augment this with *new* information. However, the system does not only have to deal with new information, even though this forms the main message of the text. The use of language frequently involves the calculated expression of *given* information to provide a context in which the message can be economically conveyed. This usually involves reference to previously-mentioned objects or situations as a preliminary to adding further informaton about them. For the program, any 'given' information provided by the input must be in accord with the partial model of the world that has been built up so far. If it is not, there is usually something wrong, as 'given' information expresses presuppositions for the communication it occurs in to be interpretable. It follows that the checking of 'given' information is an important guide when ambiguity presents itself—a possible line of analysis that leads to violated presuppositions can be abandoned immediately. Because of this advantage, we use not only the 'given' information provided explicitly by the text but we also generate extra presuppositions as 'semantic checks' on the appropriateness of the analysis. In summary, 'given' information, whatever its source, is a valuable source of *constraints* on possible interpretations. These constraints are propositions that the program must show to be true in order to validate the current interpretation. If a constraint cannot be satisfied, then it is necessary to reject the current analysis and try another possible interpretation. We will look at constraints in more detail in Chapter 3.

In this discussion, we are employing the distinction between 'given' and 'new' information as used by Haviland and Clark [Haviland and Clark 74] following from a distinction made by Halliday [Halliday 67]. They define 'given' information as 'what the listener is expected to know already' and 'new' information as 'what the listener is not expected to know already', proposing this distinction as the basis of a human language comprehension strategy. There is no universal agreement about this terminology—Chafe [Chafe 76] would probably use the words 'definite' and 'indefinite' to express this difference. Certainly there is a correlation between what is called 'given' information here and the use of the definite article, but this is not exact. Moreover, it seems unnatural to characterise the information provided by a clause as 'definite' or 'indefinite', since these terms are usually associated only with noun phrases. Because of this, we will use the terminology of Haviland and Clark, whatever its weaknesses.

The given/new distinction is a distinction on how information is used and is essentially independent of the content of that information. Thus it is possible to use 'dictionary meanings' of words (involving expansion in terms of simple semantic operations leading to Predicate Calculus assertions) which can be used in either way. As a simple example, one 'meaning' of the word 'rope' when applied to an object X might be the assertions 'linesegment(X)' and 'massive(X)' (X is a line with mass). These could either represent information to be added to the world model (in the context 'a rope is suspended from a fixed peg' when X would be the name of a new object) or represent constraints to be satisfied (in the context 'the rope weighs 10 lbs' where X would be a variable to be instantiated with the required object name). Because of this independence of given/new with 'dictionary meaning', the same routines can be used to generate assertions in both situations, and the use of the assertions need not be considered, except at the very lowest levels.

To determine how information is to be used at any point, our program uses the concept of *environments* for pieces of analysis. The idea is that the current environment specifies whether a fragment of text under consideration is providing 'given' or 'new' information. An environment will normally extend over a complete noun phrase or clause. In our program, environments are established by simple syntactic criteria.† In the example, the program operates in a 'new' environment except when it is dealing with the internal structure of 'the smooth table'. The general problem of determining given/new status of information is hard. Our syntactic strategy is simply a crude solution introduced so that we can bypass the issue of deciding given/new status.

Although it is inappropriate to investigate the details of particular semantic operations here, the above discussion indicates some assumptions that we are making about semantic operations in general. The purpose of a semantic operation is to generate assertions—either 'given' or 'new', according to the current environment. Apart from these, an operation will

---

† To simplify slightly, the definite article is taken to introduce a 'given' and the indefinite article a 'new' environment. However, see Appendix IV for some exceptions.

generate some assertions that are always 'given'—these are the semantic checks on or preconditions for its correctness. Because of this, semantic operations need to have two basic actions available:

1. To generate assertions with the status 'given' or 'new', according to the current environment.
2. To generate assertions with the status 'given'.

These two actions are illustrated in a simplified semantic operation for the word 'smooth' (Fig. 2.4).

Semantic operation: 'smooth'

When applied to an object X, yields assertions

      isa(surface,X)   ('semantic check"—always 'given')
      coeff(X,zero)   ('given' or 'new' according to environment)

Fig. 2.4–Semantic operation for 'smooth'

2.6 The Simplest Case

Let us now consider what happens in the simplest possible case of noun phrase interpretation—when each noun phrase introduces a single new object. The idea is that we will try to retain the simplicity of the system that works for this case, whilst gradually introducing more and more sophisticated features to cope with the obvious drawbacks. In this simplest situation, finding referents is trivial—the system can create a new model symbol for each phrase and does not have to worry about the possibility that two symbols might represent the same object. Moreover, since uncertainties such as we have discussed do not arise (there are no propositions about sets), semantic operations can generate assertions about completely specified objects. There are no obstacles to an early, incremental semantic analysis from this direction.

In this simplest case, 'new' assertions represent atomic propositions to be added to the database. From here they can be used in whatever inferences the system decides to make. 'Given' assertions also have a very simple interpretation. Since constraints generated in such a basic system can only mention well-defined single objects, they represent atomic propositions that must be true if the analysis is to be valid. There can be no uncertainty about whether they are true—the database and the inference rules must be able to give a firm answer.

We now show in more detail the steps that the computer program goes through in processing the sentence:

A particle of mass b rests on a smooth table.

The actual trace of the program running is to be found in Appendix VI.

Analysis of noun phrase 'a particle of mass b':
    'particle'—
        Environment is 'new', so
            new referent 'particle1' introduced.
        Semantic   operation 'particle' applied to 'particle1':
            'new' assertions 'isa(particle,particle1)'
            and 'hasname(particle,particle1)' generated.
    'of mass b'—
        Semantic   operation 'mass' applied to 'particle1':
            'given' assertion 'thasprop(particle1,mass)'
            (particle1 must be capable of having a mass)
            generated—succeeds.
            Environment is 'new', so
            new object 'mass1' introduced.
            'new' assertion 'mass(particle1,mass1,period1)'
            generated.
        Semantic   operation 'measures b' applied to 'mass1':
            'given' assertion 'not(measure(mass1,*,*))'
            generated ('mass1' must not already be known)
            —succeeds.
            'new' assertion 'measure(mass1,b,arbs)' generated.
The following is placed in the 'subject' role for the clause—
    type: physobj (physical object), value: particle1

Analysis of verb group 'rests':
The following is placed in the 'main verb' role for the clause—
    verb: rest, attributes: [singular,active, ...]

Analysis of prepositional phrase 'on a smooth table':
    Analysis of noun phrase 'a smooth table':
        'table'—
            Environment is 'new', so
                new referent 'table1' introduced.
            Semantic operation 'table' applied to 'table1':
                'new' assertions' isa(surface,table1)' and
                'hasname(table,table1)' generated.
        'smooth'—
            Semantic operation 'smooth' applied to 'table1':
                'given' assertion 'thasprop(table1,coeff)'
                generated ('table1' must be able to have
                a coefficient of friction)—succeeds.
                Environment is 'new', so
                new object 'coeff1' introduced.

'new' assertion 'coeff(table1,coeff1,period1)'
generated.
'given' assertion 'not(measure(coeff1,*,*))'
generated (the coefficient of friction must not
already be known)—succeeds.
'new' assertion 'measure(coeff1,0,arbs)' generated.
The following is put in a 'prepositional phrase'
role for the clause—
    prep: on, type: physobj (physical object), value: table1

Semantics for the main verb 'rest' now invoked.
This involves invoking the semantics of the preposition 'on'.
            Semantic operation 'on' applied to 'particle1' and 'table1':
                'given' assertion 'not(tshape(table1,point))'
                generated ('table1' must not have the shape of a
                point)—succeeds.
                Environment is 'new', so
                new object 'point1' introduced.
                'new' assertion 'point_of(table1,point1)' generated.
                'new' assertion 'contact(particle1,point1,period1)'
                generated.

The model of assertion generation allows semantic analysis to produce
meaning in small pieces as the text is read. If all noun phrases have a simple
character, this can work without being threatened by those examples of
uncertainty. In fact, we are able to keep to this basic model even when the
representation has developed to encompass various kinds of partially-
specified entities. The main changes that are necessary are for the inference system to use an extra level of knowledge about the entities and for a
stage of semantic preprocessing to be introduced between the syntactic
routines and the semantic operations. This is what has been done in our
program.

Chapter 3

SINGULAR REFERENCE EVALUATION

3.1 Reference Evaluation and Early Semantic Analysis

In Chapter 1, we saw some of the problems with finding the referent of a definite noun phrase when the phrase has just been read. The essential point was that such an approach would not allow reference evaluation to be influenced by important contextual factors. There only seemed to be two plausible solutions:

— first, we could postpone reference evaluation until some very late stage. This would amount to giving up the idea of early semantic analysis. It is not even clear that an appropriate point could be picked, by which all the relevant information would always be available.
— second, we could carry out early reference evaluation anyway. In this case, we would inevitably be forced into making early decisions on inadequate evidence and many of these would be wrong. Hence we would have to accept backtracking as an important part of the processing.

Fortunately the situation is not as bad as it looks. Much of semantic analysis can proceed with only partial knowledge about referents and it is often possible to keep several options for a referent open for some time. This chapter will present a mechanism for carrying out *incremental* reference evaluation which allows semantic operations to manipulate partially-evaluated references, both for adding 'new' information and for testing 'given' information. It is possible to make this general and relatively efficient by using 'filtering' algorithms such as that used by Waltz [Waltz 72] for finding line labellings in drawings. In order to see the applicability of these techniques, however, it is first necessary to view reference evaluation as a classical constraint satisfaction problem.

3.2   Constraints and Reference Evaluation

Reference evaluation is the task of deciding which object(s) in the world a given phrase refers to, and can be seen as the process of instantiating a variable with an appropriate value. Many factors influence what possible instantiations can be considered—these act as constraints on the value of the referent. In our basic framework, constraints take the form of 'given' assertions—preconditions for the analysis to be meaningful. Through the generation of 'given' assertions, a complex network of constraints on the values of references is produced. It is this that must be manipulated to yield a globally acceptable solution for each reference.† Before we investigate how the mechanisms work in more detail, let us consider briefly where constraints arise in natural language analysis. There are three kinds of constraints that are of importance to reference evaluation:

1. Constraints that arise directly from the meaning of the text. Every referring phrase provides some information to narrow down the set of possible referents. Thus 'the particle of mass 3 lbs' can refer only to something that is a particle and has a mass of 3 lbs. At worst, the information given may only be minimal—the only immediate constraints on the referent of 'it' are that it be an inanimate object that appears in the current discourse context.
2. Constraints generated by 'semantic checks'. At various points of the analysis, semantic routines will wish to carry out complex operations on referents of phrases (such as predicating relationships between them). These operations may have associated 'preconditions' that must be satisfied for the operations to be 'well-formed' or 'meaningful'. These 'semantic checks' are constraints on possible analysis paths—a hypothesised line of analysis can be rejected if its preconditions are not satisfied. Thus, in particular, these checks can be viewed as constraints on possible referents of the phrases involved. As an example, if the phrase 'its ends' appears in a sentence, semantic routines will eventually have to consider which precise objects the ends of 'it' are. As a precondition to this, 'it' must refer to something belonging to a class of objects that can have ends. Because of this, 'it' could never refer to a particle or a pulley, for example.

---

† Notice that we are taking a very simple approach here. Seeing reference evaluation solely as a constraint satisfaction problem involves only seeing factors that cause candidates to be *rejected*. The work of Wilks [Wilks 75] on 'preference semantics' has shown how important it is also to consider factors providing evidence *for* candidates (how one candidate may be *preferred* over another). See Section 3.6.2 for a discussion of this.

3. Constraints derived from the syntactic analysis. Syntactic considerations are known to sometimes yield coreference and disjoint reference information. For instance, the referent of 'him' in 'John hated him' cannot be the same as the referent of 'John' (if it were, the sentence would have to be 'John hated himself'). In fact, we will not say any more about constraints of this kind in this book.

As an example of what constraints might arise in practice, consider the referent of 'the particle' in

The particle moves from A to B with a velocity of 3 ft/sec.

This must be a particle because of the explicit definitional information. It must, however, also be capable of the motion described (it cannot be fixed, located at B, moving with velocity 4 ft/sec, and so on). Whereas the 'particle' constraint is given directly by the text to narrow down the set of possible referents, these other constraints are not to be found in the text at all. Instead they are necessary preliminaries before the 'new' information conveyed can be properly assimilated. Both sets of constraints must be satisfied in order for the sentence to be meaningful. It can be seen from this example that constraints on a referent can arise in several different places in the analysis. Here, the fact that the object must be a particle comes from the noun phrase itself. However, the fact that it cannot be located at B must follow from the analysis of the verb 'move' and the prepositional phrase 'to B'. Also, the fact that it cannot have some other velocity than that given comes from the analysis of the adverbial phrase 'with . . . ft/sec'.

Incremental reference evaluation recognises and builds on the fact that constraints on a referent may arise from many sources. Hence it is foolish to try to finish off the evaluation of a reference at some arbitrary point. Rather, semantic analysis should be able to use all the information provided, but still proceed with only incomplete knowledge of a referent. In order to carry out incremental reference evaluation it is necessary to have representations of partially-evaluated references and to be able to perform semantic operations with these. We will now look at this in more detail.

3.3 Representation of Unevaluated References

If semantic routines are to be able to handle unevaluated references in the same ways as other entities in the world model, there must (at a superficial level) be no significant difference between the ways in which these are represented. Thus, since 'new' objects are given symbols such as 'particle1', 'table2' to represent them in assertions this must take place for definite references too. Each singular definite phrase will give rise to a new symbol that 'represents' whatever is referred to by the phrase. Since at a deeper level there are basic differences between how the two kinds of entities are to be treated, those for definite references must be distinguished in some way. This is done in the computer program by assigning them symbols 'ref(1)', 'ref(2)', 'ref(3)', etc. For the normal manipulations of semantic operations (generating 'given' and 'new' assertions) it is possible to abstract from these differences; for deciding quite how a 'given' or 'new' assertion is to be processed, however, it may be necessary to take the differences into account. As an illustration of this, consider the difference between the two sentences:

A particle lies on a table.
The particle lies on a table.

In the first of these, the subject noun phrase gives rise to a new world model entity, represented by the symbol 'particle1' say. In the second we obtain a reference entity, say 'ref(1)', for 'the particle'. The semantic operation for the situation when an object X lies on an object Y (in a 'new' environment) might generate a 'given' assertion 'isa(physobj,X)' (X must be a physical object) and a 'new' assertion 'on(X,Y)'. The form of the assertions generated will be the same regardless as to whether X is 'particle1' or 'ref(1)'. However, satisfying the constraint 'isa(physobj,particle1)' involves a simple check on particle1; satisfying 'isa(physobj,ref(1))' involves eliminating candidates for 'the particle' that are not physical objects.

Our system keeps special information so that it can appropriately deal with these low-level operations on referents. As the text is read, more and more information will accumulate about the 'real identity' of each 'ref' entity. For each such entity the system keeps a record of the state of its evaluation with the following components:

— a candidate set;
— a set of constraints which the referent must satisfy;
— a number, expressing the minimum number of candidates that must be valid.

The candidate set contains the world model entities that the phrase might still refer to. These are the entities which have satisfied all the constraints on the referent encountered so far. Many constraints simply cause this set to be reduced and need not subsequently be recorded with the reference entity. Others have to be stored for possible reconsideration later, as we shall see. The candidate set will be given an initial value when the first constraint on the reference appears and will gradually become smaller as candidates are eliminated. The use of candidate sets reduces the necessity to reapply constraints, although it does presuppose that candidate sets need never be unmanageably large.† In association with the candidate set it is useful to keep an indicator of the minimum number of candidates that are expected to be valid. For a singular reference this is 1, for plural references 2 or more.

---

† For an alternative approach where constraints are applied more selectively and candidates do not have to be kept explicitly, see [Mellish 83].

Whenever a 'given' assertion containing the name of a reference entity is generated, it must be considered whether all the current candidates are still valid. We must reconsider each candidate in turn in the light of the extra constraint provided. When this has been done, the candidate set has, in general, become smaller. If the number of candidates left by a constraint has fallen below the minimum number, backtracking must occur; if the numbers have become equal then the referent has been finally established; otherwise the referent may still need further specification. Because constraints can cause failure even when they are applied to these partially-specified objects, a reasonable level of semantic guidance is maintained in spite of the indefiniteness implied by the approach. Although the idea of keeping several options open in parallel suggests a very loose control of parsing options, it is still possible for these semantic constraints to have a strong influence on the analysis. In particular, this means that we can still use the kinds of semantic checks used by Winograd and Novak (Section 1.3.1).

What does it mean when a 'new' assertion about a reference entity is generated? Consider what happens in an example such as:

> It is smooth.   (3.1)

when the 'new' information about the referent of 'it' (that it is smooth) is processed. Since there will probably be several candidates for the pronoun referent, this information is about an entity (a reference entity) that is not completely defined. If the value of the reference were known, then this would be equivalent to making the assertion about that value. But otherwise it is not so clear what the interpretation should be. We have taken the ascription of a property (e.g. smoothness) to a partially-specified referent as the rather vague assertion that 'whatever is referred to in the phrase has the property'. This has a similarity with the attributive interpretation of definite descriptions described by Donnellan [Donnellan 71]. Donnellan considers statements such as 'Smith's murderer is insane' in circumstances when the referent is not known. It the context of the computer program, the vague assertion mentioned has immediate consequences in terms of what statements might possibly be true. The property could possibly hold of any one of the candidates for the reference (i.e. any of the candidates might be smooth). Our knowledge of the possibilities will change as the candidate set gets reduced. Thus the 'meaning' of the assertion does not change but different amounts of outside knowledge allow more or less concrete consequences to be deduced from it. This must be handled by a special inference rule (Chapter 7).

3.4 Imposing Constraints

When a 'given' assertion is generated, it provides a check on the validity of the current analysis path. If the constraint can be satisfied then all is well; otherwise the system must backtrack to a previous choice. The situation is

more complicated when the assertion involves partially-evaluated references, because of the extra degrees of freedom possible. In such cases the
constraint may be satisfied by some candidates but not by others. We can
thus 'force' the constraint to hold by eliminating the failed candidates.
Because of the retained ambiguity of the reference, there is some extra
play available before a failure condition has to be generated. Of course,
sometimes there will be no acceptable candidates under the criterion given,
in which case a failure occurs anyway. The basic mechanism is still a simple
success/failure system, but the choice to allow a constraint to hold has
side-effects on what must be true about the references involved.

The rest of this section gives an informal description of an algorithm for
imposing constraints. This algorithm, which is used by our computer program, is presented formally in Appendix I. It is highly reminiscent of already
existing 'filtering' algorithms (see Section 3.8).

When a 'given' assertion is produced, there are three things to be done:

1. Determine which reference entities are mentioned in it. (This is simply
   done, because their names are distinguished.)
2. 'Filter' the candidate set of each such reference, to take into account the
   new constraint.
3. Investigate the repercussions of all changes made to candidate sets for
   the other references that might be affected.

If the constraint only involves one reference entity, the initial filtering step
is simple. It suffices to run through the candidate set, substituting candidates for the reference, and attempting to satisfy each of the resulting
assertions separately. If the attempt succeeds, the candidate can be kept;
otherwise it must be rejected. After the whole set has been processed, it is
necessary to check that there are enough candidates left to come up to the
minimum number for the reference—if not, failure can occur immediately.

If the constraint involves more than ne reference, more complicated
manoeuvres are necessary. Such a constraint means that the values of
several references are dependent on one another. Thus, if we later get
some more information about one of them then this may have immediate
consequences on what we know about the others. Moreover, a candidate
for one need not be considered if there are no candidates for the others
that allow the common constraint to be satisfied. Hence filtering the candidates of one leads necessarily to considering the candidates of the others.
These complexities are probably best illustrated by an example:

Let 'p1', 'p2' and 'p3' represent particles, 't1' and 't2' tables and 'z'
something else, with the following extra information known:

contact(p1,t1)
contact(p2,t2)
contact(p3,z)
shape(t2,circle)

That is, each particle is in contact with a different object. Two of these are tables, and one of the tables is circular. In such a context, the phrases 'the particle' and 'the table' will give rise to reference entities, 'ref(1)' and 'ref(2)' say, with candidate sets {p1,p2,p3} and {t1,t2} respectively. If in addition the two phrases occur in a context such as 'the particle which touches the table', then the following 'given' assertions will be generated:

contact(ref(1),ref(2))

As a result, both sets will be filtered. If we proceeded completely independently for the two references, no candidates would be rejected—'p1', 'p2' and 'p3' can all appear as first arguments of 'contact' assertions; 't1' and 't2' can both appear as second arguments. However, the constraint is more than two simultaneous unary constraints. In addition it specifies that we only want to accept a candidate X for 'ref(1)' if contact(X,Y) can be satisfied for some Y which is a valid candidate for 'ref(2)' (and vice versa). However, if 'p3' substitutes for X in the assertion then there is no candidate Y for 'ref(2)' such that the constraint holds. Hence 'p3' must be rejected. All other candidates remain, so the situation is now:

ref(1) one of {p1, p2}
ref(2) one of { t1, t2}

Another 'given' assertion:

shape(ref(2),circle)

(which would arise if we found out later that 'the table' had to be circular) now causes 't1' to be rejected as a candidate for 'ref(2)'.

Unfortunately, this is as far as we can go, given the mechanisms so far described. The algorithm must do more than this in order to make full use of the information provided. Because 'ref(2)' has become further constrained, 'ref(1)' (which is dependent on it because of the 'contact' constraint) should be reconsidered. The 'shape' assertion is no help in this—what we need to do is revive the 'contact' one and hence correctly reject 'p1' as a candidate.

The example shows that 'given' assertions involving multiple references cannot necessarily be used up and forgotten immediately. The state of candidate sets is not enough to summarise all the information known—some of the constraints must be stored as well, ready to be reapplied. The example also illustrates the necessity of considering the other references when a complex constraint is used to filter a candidate set.

Once the initial filtering for a 'given' assertion has been done (and complex constraints stored as necessary) the repercussions of any changes must be followed up. These may bring about further changes with their own repercussions, and so the propagation of changes may continue for

several passes before either a stable situation is reached or a failure is
generated. How is it ascertained what repercussions need to be considered
at any point? Whenever a candidate for a reference is rejected, all the
references which share constraints with that reference may be affected.
Thus these can be placed in a set of references to be reconsidered. The
algorithm simply involves working through this set, filtering the candidates
of the references, until the set is empty. Each time a reference is reconsidered, its candidate set is filtered using the stored constraints containing
that reference.

3.5   Some More Complex Examples

The mechanisms that have been presented for handling constraints involving unevaluated references are very general and this generality is unlikely
to be needed for understanding most coherent text. Most simple sentences
do not involve complex relationships between referents and do not need
intricate inferences for their disambiguation. To indicate that the full generality of the methods can indeed be useful in some cases, we will now
present a couple of examples.

   The first example serves to motivate informally the idea of constraint
propagation in reference evaluation.

> Into an open box is placed a wedge
> with half its horizontal dimensions.
> It extends 3 in above the top
> and also holds an inelastic ball.

If we concentrate on the second sentence, there are two references to
resolve—'it' (the box or the wedge?) and 'the top' (the top of the wedge, or
of the box?). Let us assume that these give rise to 'ref(1)' and 'ref(2)'
respectively. The first of the two conjoined clauses 'It extends 3 in above
the top' expresses a relationship between 'ref(1)' and 'ref(2)'—the former
extends 3 inches above the latter. However, nothing can extend 3 inches
above its own top. Thus we can generate a 'not top of constraint' involving
'ref(1)' and 'ref(2)'. We can illustrate this constraint diagrammatically with
a line between 'ref(1)' and 'ref(2)':

In diagrams of this sort, we will use labelled arcs to show where referents
are dependent on one another, and hence in what directions further information about one referent can have ramifications. In spite of this constraint, there is still not enough information to resolve the references at this
point. It is possible for 'ref(1)' to be the box and 'ref(2)' the top of the
wedge. Or 'ref(1)' could be the wedge and 'ref(2)' the top of the box. The
second clause introduces a relationship between 'ref(1)' and a new object,

'ball1' say. This imposes restrictions on 'ref(1)'—in order that it can hold something, it must be a container. This is a constraint that only involves 'ref(1)':

   isa(container,ref(1))

In the diagrammatic form, we show this as an arc from 'ref(1)' to itself. So we now have the following constraints:

Investigating this new constraint reveals that the only valid candidate for 'ref(1)' is the box. Following up the consequences of this, the only valid candidate for 'ref(2)' is the top of the wedge, because of the 'not part of' constraint. So the extra constraint on 'ref(1)' leads to the eventual disambiguation of 'ref(2)'. This is the power of constraint satisfaction at work.

Here is a more detailed example of constraints being used in the understanding of a mechanics problem. The following comes from a mechanics textbook [Loney 39]. In this case, the techniques of constraint propagation allow an awkward reference problem to be resolved in a pleasing way.[†]

   A uniform rod . . . is supported . . . by a string
   . . . attached to its ends.   (3.2)

The description of this example will have to be confined to a brief treatment of the reference evaluation aspects, because the treatment of sets has not yet been discussed. The problem here is in the identification of 'it', which could initially refer to either the rod or the string. However, we would like semantic checks to allow only the former, since an object cannot be said to be attached to a part of itself (the statement that a string is attached to its own ends would be anomalous).

In order to explain how this example is treated by the program, it is necessary first of all to indicate how the interpretation of a complex noun phrase such as 'its ends' takes place. We take a fairly conventional view here—that there is a rule in the 'grammar' that says something like

   NP → NP[+poss] N

That is, one form of a noun phrase consists of the possessive form of a noun phrase followed by a noun. Corresponding to the syntactic rule is a semantic rule which states that the referent of the complex NP is the result of applying some operation to the referent of the embedded NP. The exact operation is specified by the noun N. Thus in the interpretation of a phrase

---

† A trace of the computer program running on this example is given in Appendix VI.

such as 'its ends' there are actually 2 referents to be obtained—the referent
of 'its' and the referent of 'its ends'.

When the word 'its' is encountered, the program sets up a new reference,
'ref(1)', to represent the object described. This has as candidates the only
two singular objects that have been mentioned, the rod and the string:

  ref(1) one of {rod1,string1}

say. The next manoeuvre is to obtain the referent of 'its ends' by applying
the 'ends' semantic operation to 'ref(1)'. This provides various constraints,
which both candidates pass (both rods and strings can have ends). This
semantic operation also ensures that the ends of each candidate are known
and then sets up two new references to be the left and right ends of the
unknown object. To establish the dependency of the end references on the
original reference, the 'given' assertions

  end(ref(1),ref(2),left)
  end(ref(1),ref(3),right)

are produced. Thus 'ref(2)' stands for 'its left end' and 'ref(3)' for 'its right
end'; each of these has two possible candidates.

The main constituents of the relative clause ('. . . attached to its ends')
have now been interpreted and preliminary referents obtained, and so the
processing of the main verb semantics can take place. This predicates
attachment between the string and the ends, which decomposes into two
operations, one for each end.

Now the semantic operation for attachment is called, firstly with the
string ('string1') and 'ref(3)' as the objects to be attached. This corresponds to the relationship that would be derived from 'the string is attached
to its right end'. The operation will eventually generate 'new' assertions
involving the predicate 'fixed_contact'. One of the criteria for the acceptability of a statement that two objects are in contact is that they must be
'separable'. This expresses a combination of physical and pragmantic constraints. Two objects are considered 'separable' if it is conceivable that they
could be moved relative to one another. For instance, it is not physically
possible for the two ends of a rigid rod to be in contact, because they are
necessarily at a fixed distance apart, and hence not 'separable'. Also, it
would be strange to say that a string is in contact with some part of itself,
because such a proposition would be obviously true.† In this case, the
string and its part are not separable, because they are neessarily fixed
together. To express the separability constraint, the semantic operation
generates a 'given' assertion

  separable(string1,ref(3))

---

† This is appealing to something like the Gricean [Grice 75] maxim of quantity—that a
  contribution to a conversation is expected to be 'neither more nor less than is required'.

The main constraints existing at this point are shown diagrammatically in Fig. 3.1.

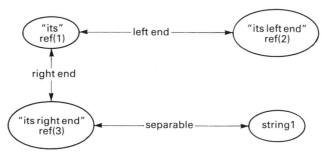

Fig. 3.1 – Constraints for 'the string is attached to its right end'

In order to satisfy this last constraint, the system attempts to prove this proposition with the right ends of the string and the rod substituted for 'ref(3)'. This succeeds for the right end of the rod but not for that of the string, because an object is not separable from a part of itself. Hence the right end of the string can be rejected as a candidate of 'ref(3)'. The first part of satisfying the constraint has now finished (an initial filtering has been carried out on all the reference entities appearing in the assertion). Now repercussions of any changes must be followed up. The only change has been in the candidate set for 'ref(3)', and this can immediately affect only those references sharing constraints with it—that is, 'ref(1)', the original 'it' reference. Filtering the candidate set of 'ref(1)' using the 'end' constraints now rejects 'string1' because 'string1' only satisfies the 'right end' condition if its right end is a candidate of 'ref(3)'; the rod now remains as the only valid candidate.

In this example, the constraints imposed on the right ends have propagated to affect a completely different referent (the referent of 'its'). This could not be done in conventional reference evaluation systems. Because the options for 'its' are held open and later constraints only indirectly concerning the reference are allowed to propagate back, this awkward reference problem can be solved.

However, the story is not yet over. The change in the candidate set of 'ref(1)' now causes repercussions for both 'ref(2)' and 'ref(3)' to be considered (both share constraints with it). Consideration of 'ref(3)' yields no more changes, but 'ref(2)' can now lose the left end of the string as a candidate. This change in 'ref(2)' causes 'ref(1)' to be reconsidered, but no more changes are forthcoming.

With the separability constraint satisfied, the semantic routine can confidently produce 'new' assertions about the attachment of 'string1' to 'ref(3)' (details will not be given here). When the attachment of 'string1' to 'ref(2)' is considered, the new constraint

separable(string1,ref(2))

is trivially satisfied because the only remaining candidate of 'ref(2)' is the
left end of the rod. There are no changes to candidate sets (and no repercussions). With all of the uncertainties resolved, the rest of the semantic
analysis is comparatively straightforward.

3.6 Limitations

Having indicated the usefulness of treating reference evaluation as a constraint satisfaction process, we should now consider some limitations of the
approach.

3.6.1 Other Interfaces to the Database

The successful use of constraint satisfaction algorithms to deal with reference evaluation and semantic checks relies on the fact that the main activity of semantic operations is forming 'given' and 'new' assertions. However, it may not be appropriate to see all the interfaces to the database in
this way. Sometimes a semantic operation may require the ability to ask a
question rather than demand that a constraint be satisfied. For instance,
the interpretation of the modifier '6 inch' applied to an object may depend
crucially on what kind of object it is—'a 6 inch rod' is probably a rod 6
inches long, but 'a 6 inch cable' could well be a cable 6 inches in diameter.
We would like to be able to define the semantic operation for 'N inch'
something like as in Fig. 3.2.

Semantic operation: 'N inch'

    When applied to an object X, yields assertions as follows

    If 'cable_like(X)' is true, then
        diameter(X,D) and measure(D,N,inches)   ('given' or 'new')

    Otherwise
        length(X,L) and measure(L,N,inches)   ('given' or 'new')

Fig. 3.2 – Semantic operation for 'N inch'—version 1

The semantic operation needs to be able to ask the question 'Is the object
cable-like?' before it can decide which assertions to generate. According to
whether the answer is 'yes' or 'no', one set of assertions or the other will be
selected. Can such notions be accommodated in our existing system for
constraint satisfaction?

    The simplest approach to this problem seems to be to incorporate ques-
tions into our framework by pretending that they are really constraints. We
end up with two possible routes through the semantic operation and a

choice to be made between them (Fig. 3.3). If we have to apply the semantic operation to some entity 'cable1', say, the first route will only work if
the constraint that 'cable1' is cable-like is satisfiable (otherwise the constraint will fail and backtracking will hit the second possibility). Similarly,
the second route will only work if 'cable1' is not cable-like. So we can use
the success/failure mechanism of applying constraints to answer yes/no
questions about which path to follow. If we pose a question as a constraint,
we can take its successful satisfaction as the answer 'yes'; otherwise we can
take the answer to be 'no'.

Semantic operation: 'N inch'

    When applied to an object X, yields assertions

    Possibility A:
      cable_like(X)   ('given')
      diameter(X,D) and measure(D,N,inches)   ('given' or 'new')

    Possibility B:
      not(cable_like(X))   ('given')
      length(X,L) and measure(L,N,inches)   ('given' or 'new')

Fig. 3.3 – Reformulation of version 1

    Unfortunately, there are some penalties associated with seeing questions
as constraints. A yes/no question at a decision point in the analysis is
fundamentally different from a constraint. When a constraint is generated,
an attempt is always made to answer 'yes, this is true', and candidates for
unevaluated references will be rejected as necessary to achieve this. With a
question, however, there is no reason to expect either 'yes' or 'no' as an
answer. Treating it as a constraint means that we will try to force a 'yes'
answer, even if this involves rejecting some candidates for partially-
evaluated references. If there is real ambiguity, the constraint may be
allowed when it should not be, and correct candidates may be rejected in
the process. This may happen if we apply the semantic operation to a
reference entity, 'ref(3)' say, with many different kinds of candidates. In
such a situation, some candidates may be cable-like and some not. When
candidates are rejected by one of the constraints, we will have to rely on
backtracking to keep the other open as a possibility. However, only the
minimal choices are forced by the question—if in the example all the
candidates of 'ref(3)' were cables then no decision would be necessary.
    A second kind of question that a semantic operation might ask is one
where a non-trivial answer is involved. For instance, Fig. 3.4 shows a
reformulation of the 'N inch' operation where we ask instead 'What kind of
object is X?'.

Semantic operation: 'N inch'

When applied to an object X, yields assertions as follows

For the Y such that 'isa(Y,X)' is true,

If Y is 'cable' then
    diameter(X,D) and measure(D,N,inches)   ('given' or 'new')
Otherwise if Y is 'string' then
    length(X,L) and measure(L,N,inches)   ('given' or 'new')

Otherwise . . .

Fig. 3.4 – Semantic operation for 'N inch'—version 2

In this case, we introduce an assertion containing a variable ('for what Y is X of type Y?'), which becomes instantiated through a deductive process. Suppose we have a referent 'cable1' and wish to apply the modifier '6 in' to it. In order to determine what the appropriate meaning is, we need to ask what kind of object 'cable1' is—for what value of variable Y is

    isa(Y,cable1)

true? Now, answering this question is again very close to seeing if the assertion can be applied as a constraint (does there exist Y such that the type of 'cable1' is Y?). The only difference is that we require to know in addition what value of Y makes the assertion true. It would seem quite reasonable for the constraint satisfaction algorithm to instantiate Y as a side effect if the constraint can be satisfied. This would allow us to deal with the question as a constraint again. Thus in the program we have introduced a mechanism for instantiating variables that occur in constraints. This enables questions containing variables to be answered without the introduction of much extra machinery.

What happens in the above if there are two possible values for Y? A plausible case where this could happen would be in asking the question about an unevaluated reference:

    isa(Y,ref(3))

If 'ref(3)' has candidates of different types, what should the answer be? Here there is no single value that can instantiate Y. The value that is returned should reflect this ambiguity somehow and also have its dependency on 'ref(3)' recorded. The natural way to do this is to set up a new reference entity for Y and treat the above assertion as a constraint on its value. In this case, the answer to the question 'What kind of object is "ref(3)"?' is something like 'ref(4)'.

So questions containing variables can be 'answered' in some sense without a great change in the existing mechanisms. However, an answer such as 'ref(4)' is not in itself very informative—we need to be able to access more specific information sometimes. Fortunately we can do this by formulating even more constraints on the answer—could it be equal to a certain value? could it have a certain property? and so on. Bearing these comments in mind, we can again reformulate the semantic operation purely in terms of 'given' and 'new' assertions (Fig. 3.5).

Semantic operation: 'N inch'

   When applied to an object X, yields assertions as follows

   isa(Y,X)   ('given')

   Possibility A:
     Y=cable   ('given')
     diameter(X,D) and measure(D,N,inches)   ('given' or 'new')

   Possibility B:
     Y=string   ('given')
     length(X,L) and measure(L,N,inches)   ('given' or 'new')

   Possibility C:
   . . . . . .

Fig. 3.5 – Reformulation of version 2

In this section, we have seen how the normal mechanism for handling 'given' assertions is capable of handling 'questions' from semantic routines. This means that in semantic operations it is possible to deal with conditions that are not obviously constraints. Unfortunately, when questions involving unevaluated references arise, it is sometimes necessary to rely on backtracking as a last resort. This is because some parts of the semantic processing may depend for their very structure on properties of particular referents. In such cases, it may be necessary to make decisions about some references in order that the semantic analysis can proceed at all. This is a problem that would affect any approach to early semantic analysis. At least in our system the choices are postponed for as long as possible. In considering examples such as this, we have found the limits to the possibilities for postponing reference evaluation. Eventually the point comes when the options can no longer be considered in parallel.

3.6.2 Incorporating Evidence for Candidates
We mentioned earlier the fundamental simplification that our concentration on constraints makes. The function of a constraint is primarily to reject

candidates for a reference—that is, it serves only to provide evidence *against* individual candidates. In a natural-language-understanding system, we might well want to consider in addition evidence *for* individual candidates, so that we could detect when some candidate is *preferred* over its rivals. This might be useful for the following:

A. To make a final decision about a reference that has remained ambiguous for a long time. We cannot expect consistency constraints always to reject all but one of the candidates, and we must decide what to do when it appears that such an elimination will not happen. One possibility is to choose the candidate that has been mentioned most recently or is most 'in focus' ([Sidner 79], [Grosz 77]).

B. To make a decision about references by considering the relative plausibility of interpretations with various combinations of candidates. Here we might be considering *global* plausibility, as well as plausibility for references individually, and we might want to use some kind of 'preference semantics' [Wilks 75].

C. To allow referents to be *predicted* from considerations of how the individual sentences of the input fit in coherently with the subject of the discourse as a whole. Predictions might come from the firing of 'demons' [Charniak 72] or from the fitting of inputs into an active 'script' [Schank *et al.*, 75].

The problem with point A is that of knowing when to make the final decision. We saw earlier that it is *not* in general appropriate to decide at the end of the noun phrase. There are probably also examples where it is not appropriate to decide at the end of the sentence. We will argue (in Section 4.1) that a language understanding system must always be on the look-out for identities between entities in its world model. Thus establishing 'coreference' is not a process that is ever complete, and there is no theoretical reason to force decisions when there is ambiguity. From a practical point of view, however, it may be that focus criteria can lead to reliable decisions. Moreover, a program will obviously perform better at question answering or problem solving if it has resolved all the definite references in advance. Hence making decisions about some references may well be justified to some extent. We could easily extend the current system to include ordering information in the candidate sets. This would enable us to express how likely a candidate is according to focus criteria, and to make a decision quickly if it is needed.

'Preference' on a local scale can in fact be modelled by the use of constraints. If there is a proposition that we would 'prefer' to be true at some point in the analysis (e.g. the proposition that the agent of 'put' in animate), but which need not necessarily be true, we can introduce a choice point. The first alternative involves satisfying the propostion as a constraint (rejecting candidates as necessary) and the second involves satisfying its negation as a constraint. Thus only the candidates that allow the proposition to hold will be kept in the first instance; if the choice has to be remade, the others will be selected. That is, the preferred path is tried first. The first example of the use of 'questions' (Section 3.6) can, in fact, be seen as expressing a preference (that an object described by the modifier 'N inch' is cable-like) in this way.

Unfortunately, 'preference' in the global sense, as used by Wilks [Wilks 75], cannot be easily accommodated. This is because in our system all choices are cumulative—any decision that is made is a local optimisation, *given the results of the choices so far*. Thus consider the case where there is an ambiguous reference, and a preference involving it is generated. An attempt will be made to satisfy the preference, and this may involve rejecting some candidates. In the subsequent analysis, preferences may be satisfied or not, but everything must work on the assumption that the original preference was true. Only if an absolute contradiction is found will that assumption be called into question. This mechanism will not necessarily obtain the best global solution, because it might be a violation of the first preference that actually leads to a larger number of preferences being satisfied overall.

Finally, as regards point C, a system for predicting referents could be integrated with the constraint satisfaction framework presented. When a referent is predicted by such a system, it suffices to check that the predicted value is indeed in the candidate set. Then the other candidates can be rejected and any implications followed up. A system similar in some ways to this has, in fact, been implemented and is described in [Mellish 83]. If such a system wishes to test whether preconditions for the applicability of a 'script' or 'frame' are satisfied, this can be catered for in the same way as local preferences. This is, the preconditions could be treated as constraints, and reference evaluation 'pushed' if at all possible into a direction that would enable them to be satisfied. As we noted above, this mechanism of local preference would not necessarily lead to the interpretation that was the globally most plausible one.

3.7 Relation to Other Uses of Constraints

Since the evaluation of references has been seen as a constraint satisfaction problem, it is interesting to see how the approach presented here corresponds to other formulations of constraint satisfaction problems.

Mackworth [Mackworth 77] uses the notation of networks of relations to express algorithms for manipulating constraints. In his terminology, the specification of a constraint satisfaction problem can be seen as a labelled, directed graph. A node of this graph represents a variable whose value is to be determined and each arc represents a constraint that holds between the nodes that it connects. Associated with each node is a set of possible values for the variable it represents. Since Mackworth only considers unary and binary constraints, he can express all his problems as graphs without hyperarcs.

The correspondence between Mackworth's model and the reference evaluation problem is apparent. Corresponding to his nodes, we have reference entities whose 'values' are sought; corresponding to arcs we have the 'given' assertions that mutually constrain sets of references. Our candidate sets are the equivalent of his node sets. Since assertions linking more than two references are conceivable, not all our arcs are necessarily binary.

Given this basic terminology, Mackworth goes on to consider three kinds of consistency in networks—node, arc and path. These represent states where progressively more implications of the constraints are reflected in the sets associated wit the nodes. Node consistency means that each value in a node set satisfies all the unary constraints attached to that node. Arc consistency means that each value in a node set satisfies each of the constraints on the node in such a way that the values instantiated for other nodes are in fact elements of the required node sets. Path consistency is an extension of arc consistency that considers paths of several arcs simultaneously.

How important are these kinds of consistency in the reference evaluation task? Although we have not made detailed investigations, it is anticipated that merely considering node consistency will clear up reference ambiguities in almost all examples. However, the example of Section 3.5 (repeated here for convenience):

> A uniform rod . . . is supported . . . by a string
> . . . attached to <u>its</u> ends.   (3.2)

shows that arc consistency can also be needed. Whether examples can be found that require consideration of path consistency or even more stringent criteria (such as are discussed by Freuder [Freuder 78]) remains to be seen. None have arisen to date.

Node consistency in a fixed network can be achieved in a preliminary pass. This is reflected in our algorithm by the fact that constraints involving only one reference are only kept for as long as it takes to do an initial filtering of the candidate set, whereas all other constraints are saved for possible later use. Arc consistency can be obtained by a variety of algorithms. The one described here (which is implemented in the computer program) is similar to that used by Waltz [Waltz 72] in his program to analyse drawings of scenes with shadows. Path consistency has not been discussed here (although the computer program can be asked to attain this through a rather crude algorithm).

The fact that we are using the Waltz filtering algorithm for reference evaluation does suggest that the structure of this problem might be quite similar to that of labelling drawings of scenes. This is supported by a number of observations. Firstly, although Waltz is interested in obtaining the set of possible labellings of the scene, and achieving network consistency is only part of his task, in practice it dominates the task. This is because the other part of the Waltz task, which involves enumerating unambiguous solutions, is unnecessary in most cases. Similarly, in reference evaluation the constraints should produce a unique solution except in pathological cases. Secondly, although the line-labelling task can be presented as a fixed network given in advance, Waltz builds it up incrementally, adding new nodes and arcs just as we add new references and constraints. A slight difference is that the reference evaluation mechanism has to offer the possibility of rejecting an addition to the network. This is because the search tree for parsing may generate incorrect hypotheses that are manifested in unsatisfiable constraints. Thus the addition to the network of a constraint that destroys consistency must lead to a failure condition. In labelling the lines of a scene, one expects never to encounter such a situation, although one could envisage a system where it would cause low-level line-finding procedures to look for alternative solutions.

Constraint propagation techniques have not just been used in computer vision programs. Other applications have included solving puzzles [Burstall 69] and database retrieval [Grossman 76]. Winston [Winston 77] suggests using constraint satisfaction as a way of tackling tasks in natural language understanding, such as filling case slots, but this does not seem to have been implemented. This idea of using constraints to tackle reference evaluation is, however, original with us, as far as we can determine.

3.8 Summary

This chapter has presented a mechanism for *incremental* reference evaluation. This mechanism provides the following facilities:

—Semantic operations taking place at widely differing times can all be used to constrain the value of a single reference.
— Most semantic operations can proceed using information from partially-evaluated as well as fully-evaluated references. Their manipulations will remain valid when more information arrives and their results will not have to be altered.
— These facilities do not in general require premature decisions to be made about references.

The incremental evaluation mechanism is suggested by viewing reference evaluation as a classical constraint satisfaction problem and building on algorithms used in computer vision by Waltz [Waltz 72] and Mackworth [Mackworth 77].

Chapter 4

INDEFINITE NOUN PHRASES

In this chapter, we consider some of the problems with the early semantic interpretation of *indefinite* noun phrases. These problems are:

1. To some extent, the problems that arise when a phrase may be talking about something already known about (as occurs regularly with definite phrases).
2. The problems of ascertaining what kind of set is referred to when cardinality information is lacking or quantifiers may appear later in the sentence.

In order to confront these problems, we present:

1. An approach to 'coreference' in terms of the representation of coextension information between intensional entities in the world model. This generalises the previous use of 'reference entities' and allows for other kinds of identification to take place.
2. An approach to the representation of vaguely-defined sets using the idea of 'typical elements'. This involves the use of *dependency lists* to express the structure of sets represented and to provide a clear semantics for propositions about typical elements.

Before we look at the problems in detail, we should consider the basic question—what are indefinite noun phrases for? A simple model of declarative sentences sees them as *introducing* objects that exist in the world. Thus in:

> A light inextensible string, passing over a smooth
> fixed pulley, carries . . . (4.1)

(from [Humphrey 57]) the normal interpretation is that that both the string and the pulley are objects that the reader is not assumed to be already acquainted with. The use of the indefinite article signals that the reader's world model must be augmented approximately.

It is this simple view of indefinite noun phrases that we will take as the basis of the approach developed. Unfortunately, this view is not adequate to cover all uses of indefinite noun phrases. We will consider some of the problems when such a phrase may be talking about specific objects that *are* already known about or when there is local uncertainty about the size of the set being introduced. Some of the problems arising from the possibility for other uses of indefinite noun phrases will be alluded to briefly in Section 4.6.

4.1 Problems with Coextension

The simple model of indefinite noun phrases that we have mentioned assumes that the reader is not already acquainted with the referent of such a phrase. In real interactions between human beings this assumption can be incorrect if the speaker is not fully aware of the hearer's knowledge. Hence a sentence such as:

Mrs Jones bought a new dog yesterday.

may in some situations give the hearer new information about the dog that he has already seen in Mrs Jones' window, instead of introducing a completely new object. In general, the way a speaker thinks of (and marks) information as 'given' and 'new' may not correspond directly to the way the hearer relates it to his existing world model. Thus, although a reader should make use of what is marked 'given' and 'new' in a text, he must always be aware that there may be a mismatch between his actual knowledge and the writer's model of that knowledge. In general, a process of inference is necessary to establish that two entities introduced as 'new' in different contexts correspond to the same object in the world. Existing correspondences may indeed not be established until a long time after the entities are created or may never be discovered. This presents a potential problem to early semantic interpretation, because it means that full knowledge of referents may not be obtainable by the time a noun phrase has been read. Fortunately, this does not mean that the entities can no longer be used sensibly, but only that certain information is lacking. A lot of interesting investigations and deductions can take place in the absence of total 'coextension' information. So we might hope to continue with semantic interpretation regardless. In the above example, the hearer might be acquainted with all the dogs that Mrs Jones might have bought, but might not know which she had chosen. However, he would still be able to continue the conversation with remarks such as:

I hope it is better house trained than the last one.

What relevance do these considerations have for a computer program attempting to understand natural language? It certainly means that the program must be wary of possible redundancies among the entities in its world model. Inferential processes should be able to establish correspondences independently and record them for later use. In particular, it means that there is not necessarily a simple correspondence between symbols in the world model and objects in the world. The entities represented must be considered as having intensional status; they are assumed to correspond to distinct objects, but this default may be overridden at any time. We need not worry too much about immediately relating indefinite noun phrase entities to entities already existing. Indeed, we can happily create a new world model entity for each indefinite NP. The process of establishing coextension between the world model entities is completely independent and can be treated separately.

This discussion serves to justify and further illuminate the status of reference entities in our world model. We have argued that a representation of the meaning of noun phrases cannot necessarily assume total knowledge of which entities correspond to the same object in the world. The kind of uncertainty that reference entities express is therefore quite in place. Indeed we can see the existence of reference entities as a special case of a general arrangement where information is kept about possible (extensional) correspondences between entities in the world model. Our computer program has this general capability, but it has only been explored thoroughly for the case of reference entities. One possibility is to use the ability to record possible correspondences in interpreting some meanings of the verb 'to be'. Thus in:

> The string is a̲ nylon cord of
> high tensile strength.   (4.2)

a conventional approach might consider the phrase 'a nylon . . .' to refer more to an abstract concept (or set of properties) than a concrete object. According to this view, the phrase has no 'referent' in the simplest sense of the word. The effect of the sentence is to ascribe the properties of this abstract object to the string (a concrete object). On the other hand, given the facilities of the framework developed, we can take both 'the string' and 'a nylon cord . . .' to give rise to world model entities, and the sentence as a whole to predicate coextension between them.

This section has proposed the maintenance of a world model populated by entities of an intensional nature. Associated with each entity is information about which entities it could be 'identical' to. Indefinite noun phrases give rise to entities that are initially assumed to correspond to distinct objects, whereas definite phrases give rise to entities where there is known to be redundancy. Since each phrase gives rise to a new entity in the model and coextension is dealt with as separate information, we have ended up representing 'mentions of objects', rather than real world objects themselves. The inference system must be able to use information about possible correspondences to relate information recorded in terms of one symbol to information in terms of others. This is simply a generalisation of the methods outlined in Section 3.3. We describe the appropriate part of the inference system in Chapter 7.

4.2 Problems with Numbers and Quantification

Examples (1.2) and (1.3) illustrate how the number of objects referred to in an indefinite noun phrase may not be ascertainable on a purely local basis. These examples are repeated here for convenience:

<u>Small blocks</u>, each of mass m, are clamped at the ends
and at the centre of a light rod.   (1.2)

A wooden stool 2 ft 2 in in high consists of . . .
a <u>uniform vertical leg</u> at each corner.   (1.3)

If it is not known how many objects a phrase refers to, it is not possible to reason about the individual objects. Hence it appears that local semantic analysis of indefinite noun phrases is impossible—the necessary 'concrete' referents are simply not available. However, although analysis at the level of referents may not be possible, an analysis at the noun phrase level *is* still available. Moreover, the referential nature of indefinite noun phrases means that initially this is quite adequate. An indefinite noun phrase is usually introducing objects not already known about. Hence the analysis of propositions phrased wholly in terms of indefinite phrases rarely needs to worry about consistency with the specific details of the world as known. Such propositions can only be evaluated by a consideration of their *internal* consistency, given *general* knowledge about the world. Thus we are led to consider a level of interpretation for indefinite noun phrases that is concerned with inferences of an intensional nature about the parts of the description provided. Let us see how this might be fitted into our rather 'referential' framework.

Consider the simple phrase 'a light string'. According to our basic framework, the analysis of this phrase consists of finding the referent and generating assertions about it. The former will be achieved by creating a new world model entity and giving it the properties of a string (assuming that noun phrase interpretation begins at the noun). The semantic operation for 'light' must consider the appropriateness of the property to the referent, which will be done by the generation of 'given' assertions. These constraints will be satisfied because the known properties of the referent (being a string and having no known mass) are compatible with the 'light' property. The satisfaction of these constraints can be phrased entirely as operations on the 'referent'. Nevertheless, the only information that is available is that coming from the introducing phrase itself. Hence the 'referent' of the indefinite phrase is really just acting as a way of accessing the description given ('a string') and the inferences about it can be seen as establishing the compatibility of this with an extra piece of information ('light'). So inferences about the consistency of the description in an indefinite noun phrase *can* be made using the existing machinery, given the notion of using a 'referent' to access the description. Notice, however, how the same machinery of constraint satisfaction would end up treating new properties expressed of a *definite* phrase, as in '*the string* is light'. Here, because the object is already known about, checking the appropriateness of 'light' for the referent may involve accessing information that has been provided about it over a number of sentences. This is nothing at all like checking the consistency of two descriptions.

When we come to consider a more complicated phrase such as 'some light strings', it is clear that the same problem of consistency of descriptions is involved, even though referents may not be available. Once again we can use a 'referent' as a handle to access the components of the description being formed. This referent can be treated just as any other entity in the world model—we can see it as the 'typical element' of the set referred to. The system can then make deductions about this, for evaluating the appropriateness of modifiers and so on. Note that it makes sense to reason about the typical element even if (some aspect of) the set cardinality is known—the same techniques will apply to '3 light strings', '3000 light strings', 'n light strings' and so on. The reason is that the properties say the same about each element of the set.[†] Thus it is quite safe to argue about them in a single operation—all the elements are known to behave identically under inference. Even if we think we know how many elements there are, treating each one separately simply means repeating the same work many times. In this context, a number supplied with an indefinite NP is almost irrelevant.

4.3 Dependency Lists

This section introduces the notion of *dependency lists* for representing information about typical elements introduced by indefinite noun phrases. The set of objects referred to by an indefinite NP may decompose along several independent dimensions which are brought out by the phrase and its context. For instance, consider the set of pulleys in:

A length of rope and two blocks each containing 3 pulleys
are supplied. (4.3)

In this example (from [McKenzie 60]), there are a total of six pulleys. Firstly, we are told explicitly that there are three main subsets by the number '3' in the phrase. Secondly, each subset decomposes into two elements, corresponding to the two blocks. We shall call the first kind of decomposition an 'external' decomposition, as it is explicitly marked. The

---

† That is, we are considering *distributive* properties.

second kind of decomposition arises from a dependency on a set mentioned elsewhere and is signalled by a word such as 'each' (corresponding to a universal quantifier in logic). In general, an indefinite NP entity can decompose into separate dimensions for:

1. The possible 'external' set elements.
2. Each distinct universal quantifier that governs it.

We can represent the two dimensios into which the set of pulleys decomposes by a simple diagram (Fig. 4.1).

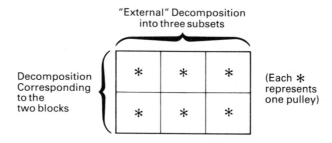

Fig. 4.1 – The set of pulleys

Although we can do a lot of work at the level of the typical element of such a set, it is unreasonable to expect that we will never have to deal with individual elements. So we must keep track of what kind of set a 'typical element' corresponds to—how it decomposes into subsets, what cardinality information is known and so on. This is the function of a dependency list. Not all of the relevant information will be immediately available, and so we will have to represent partial information that can be gradually updated.

A 'dependency list' is thus associated with each indefinite noun phrase entity.[†] This list will be able to expand as necessary to record all the separate dimensions making up the set of objects. The entity arising for the pulleys in this example has two dependencies. It has an 'external' dependency with number 3, because the phrase is plural and the number 3 is provided (we are *told* that there are three subsets). It also has a dependency with number 2 (because there are two blocks) as a result of the effect of the 'each' quantifier. The computer program makes use of a dependency list representation of this kind. Each entry in a dependency list has three components, as follows:

1. A dependency name. This is to indicate the origin of the dependency—it could be an 'external' dependency or a dependency on a particular set. The name can be used as a guide to routines for establishing quantifier scope (Section 6.1).

---

† Later we will consider dependency lists for other types of entities as well.

2. A number. This indicates the total number of subsets that the dependency creates (for 'external' this may be a number supplied in the noun phrase; for dependencies on sets this gives the cardinality of the set depended on). This information need not necessarily be known when the entry is created.
3. A 'usage' indicator. This is a flag that tells whether this dependency has been the basis of a non-trivial division into sub-classes.

The point of the 'usage indicator' in the dependency entry is to distinguish between entries that merely express information about how the set is composed, and entries which each subset created by the dependency has had to be considered separately for the purpose of some semantic operation. For instance, when we interpret '2 particles of mass b and c', we must treat the two (possibly, sets of) particles separately, because we must assert that one has mass b and the other mass c. As a result, the first, 'external' dependency of the entity will get marked 'used'. This need not happen with a phrase such as '3 particles', where the properties can be asserted of the typical element of the set as a whole (Section 6.2.1). A dependency cannot possibly be marked 'used' unless its number has been established, for it is impossible to consider the subsets separately until it is known how many there are.

The information that an indefinite noun phrase entity has an 'external' dependency is conveyed by the plurality of the phrase. A number may also be communicated at the same time ('*3000* particles'), but this information is likely to be of little importance at first when the entity can be treated as a single unit for the purpose of inferences.

In order to distinguish between the different states that an entity can be in, let an entity that has at least one 'used' dependency be called *broken*. Thus '2 particles of mass b and c' gives rise to a broken entity, but '3 particles' need not. An unbroken entity stands for the typical element of a set whose elements are currently indistinguishable.

In the examples of dependency lists given here, each entry will be shown in the form

$$(\langle name \rangle, \langle number \rangle, \langle flag \rangle)$$

with '_' representing an unknown number and 'T' and 'F' representing the possible values of the 'usage' flag ('true' and 'false'). For instance, the complete version of the dependency list of the pulleys entity is

[(external,3,F),(block1,2,F)...]

where 'block1' is the name of the blocks entity.

4.4 Semantics of Propositions about Typical Elements

Assertions formulated in terms of typical element entities must be usable by the inference system at various times in the semantic analysis. Each time there may be more concrete information about the dependencies than the time before. An indefinite noun phrase entity may start with no known dependencies, may then accumulate some as a quantifier is discovered, and finally inferences may be carried out in terms of a very specific element of the set. At each stage, the very earliest assertions made about the entity may be needed. The information embodied in the dependency list provides the basis for interpreting the assertions in the correct amount of detail each time. We must, however, provide a clear semantics for assertions about typical elements, and ensure that the interpretations will remain true whatever extra information about dependencies may later arrive.

4.4.1   Entities and Sub-entities

First of all, we will need to be able to talk abut subsets and elements of sets represented by typical elements. Given a typical element entity, we introduce into the world model entities for particular elements of the set and entities for typical elements of certain subsets. These are called *sub-entities* of the original entity. Sub-entities are created by the syntactic device of *subscripting*. This has the advantage that:

— it can always be determined *syntactically* what relation an entity has to one of its sub-entities;
— sub-entities can be used only as needed, without an explicit step of 'creation'.

Consider again the pulleys of the last section. At the point when the words '3 pulleys' have just been encountered, our representation will be as follows:

    entity: pulley1
    dep list: [(external,3,F). . .]

In this state, the entity corresponds to the typical element of a set that breaks down into three subsets. If no more dependencies arrive, these subsets will in fact contain single elements. We can talk about the second subset by using the sub-entity

    pulley1.2

Note that this may represent a single object (if 'pulley1' receives no more dependencies), or it may represent the typical element of a subset of the original set. Later on, when the relationship with the blocks has been uncovered, the situation will be:

    entity: pulley1
    dep list: [(external,3,F),(block1,2,F). . .]

and then 'pulley1.2' will represent the typical element of a set that itself breaks down into two subsets. Again, these may contain single individuals or not (according to whether more dependencies arrive). We can represent these by

    pulley1.2.1   pulley1.2.2

Notice that we add subscripts in the same order that the dependencies occur in the list. At this point, the lowest level sub-entities available are

    pulley1.1.1   pulley1.2.1   pulley1.3.1
    pulley1.1.2   pulley1.2.2   pulley1.3.2

The structure of subscripts makes it clear how each of these relates to the entities of which it is a sub-entity. Also, it is clear from the dependency list at each point which sub-entities are meaningful. For instance, it would make no sense to talk about

    pulley1.4.1   or   pulley1.2.5   or   pulley1.2.2.1

given the dependency list above, for the first two are in contradiction to the information already known about the size of the subsets. The last one makes no sense at the moment (because it may amount to making a sub-division within a single individual), but it may make sense at some later time. At any time, the dependency list determines which sub-entities are well-formed. A semantic operation can use a sub-entity allowed by the dependency list without having to explicitly 'create' an entry in the world model. Such an entity is already implicitly known to exist.

    Given an entity with more than one dependency, such as our example:

    entity: pulley1
    dep list: [(external,3,F),(block1,2,F). . .]

we can refer to the typical element of a certain kind of subset by just leaving off some subscripts. Thus

    pulley1.3

represents the third subset given by the first dependency. This is a set that divides into two subsets, each of which may have just one element. We can see this as some kind of abbreviation for

    pulley1.3.X

where X is a variable, indicating that we are not interested in the value of this subscript—only in the 'typical' value along this dimension. Looked at another way, we are interested in the typical element of the set of lowest level sub-entities of 'particle1' that have 3 as their first subscript. The possibility of using variables means that we can actually represent various other subsets, such as

    pulley1.X.2

This is the typical element of the set obtained by taking all the lowest level sub-entities of 'pulley1' which have 2 as the second subscript. If 'pulley1' now has its full complement of dependencies (so that things such as 'pulley1.1.1' represents individuals) we can display some of these subsets in a diagram (Fig. 4.2).

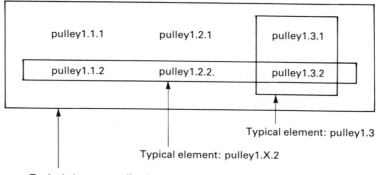

Fig. 4.2 – Subsets of pulleys

Finally, let us consider what sub-entities of an entity are appropriate when there is no cardinality information about one of the dependencies. If we have an entity such as

entity: rod1
dep list: [(external,_,F). . .]

then it would be dangerous to start considering entities such as 'rod1.3' and 'rod1.6', because they may end up contradicting the cardinality information when it arrives. So we stipulate that, when the number of a dependency is not known, the dependency list only allows sub-entities with a variable subscript in that position. Other sub-entities are simply not well formed. So in this case we can only consider the typical element

rod1.X, i.e. rod1

We will, in fact, extend this stipulation to cover cases where, even though the number is known, it can serve no useful purpose to consider non-variable subscripts. This is the case when the 'usage flag' of a dependency is 'F', indicating that the sub-entities arising from the division along this dimension are currently indistinguishable. Here, the dependency list will prevent over-specific sub-entities being considered because it is only wasteful to perform semantic operations at such a level (see Section 6.2.1).

4.4.2 Simple Assertions about Typical Elements

Now that the subscript notation is available, the semantics of assertions about typical elements can be explained. We need to say what an assertion means if it contains a name that is 'underspecified' with respect to the corresponding dependency list (that is, if it does not have enough subscripts). The details of this are embodied in an inference rule described more fully in Chapter 7, but the basic idea is that if a subscript corresponding to a dependency does not occur in the assertion then the assertion is about a typical element along this dimension. Thus

   isa(block,block1)

is equivalent to

   (X)   isa(block,block1.X)

which is equivalent to

   (Y)   (X)   isa(block,block1.X.Y)

and so on, for as long as is meaningful. This is in accordance with our abbreviatory convention that

   block1   means   block1.X   means   block1.X.Y, etc.

   There are two things to be noted at this point. Firstly, when we translate assertions involving several variables into universally quantified propositions in this way, it becomes important how we name the variables. For

   (X)   isa(block,block1.X.X)

means something completely different from

   (X)   (Y)   isa(block,block1.X.Y)

We will discuss this more in the next section. Secondly, although we have used universal quantifiers, it must be understood that the possible values of a subscript are limited by whatever cardinality and usage information is known about the relevant dependency. Thus if we have something like

   entity: particle2
   dep list: [(a,_,F)(b,2,T). . .]

then the most concrete sub-entities that can be considered are 'particle2.X.1' and 'particle2.X.2', where X is a variable.

4.4.3   More Complex Assertions

We can extend the discussion of 'underspecified' assertions to a consideration of more complex relationships involving typical elements. Consider a sentence such as:

   2 spheres are attached to 2 walls.

There are various possible interpretations of this sentence. One possibility is that each sphere is attached to each wall. This kind of relationship, where each member of one set is related to each member of another, can be handled with a simple extension of what we have discussed. If 'sphere1' and 'wall1' are appropriate typical element entities, then we can represent the situation by

   contact(sphere1,wall1)

and stipulate that this is equivalent to

   (X)   (Y)   contact(sphere1.X,wall1.Y)

To get this interpretation, we must simply avoid accidentally choosing the same variable name twice in the translation. However, sometimes we want to capture relationships between *corresponding* elements of two sets. Thus it may be that each of the spheres is attached to exactly one of the walls. We can represent this with the same assertion, given an added restriction on the possible values of subscripts. Now we require that the subscripts for the two dependencies be consistently chosen. That is, we wish

   contact(sphere1,wall1)

to be equivalent to

   (X)   contact(sphere1.X,wall1.X)

In this case, we must intentionally choose the same variable name in the two places to get the indended meaning. We will use the term *linked* to express the fact that two dependencies have been marked as corresponding in this way. Being linked together is a reflexive and symmetric relation, and in Chapter 6 we will consider some possible rules for deciding when to link dependencies together.

In conclusion, then, the meaning of an assertion involving typical elements is the same as that of the (universally quantified) formula obtained by adding variables as subscripts. The choice of variable names is determined by which dependencies are *linked* together. Subscripts corresponding to linked dependencies must use the same variable. All others must use different variables.

4.4.4 Example
To illustrate the use of dependency lists, let us briefly consider the example about the block of pulleys further. Some of the details will be omitted from the discussion because they are concerned with issues addressed in Chapters 5 and 6. Rewriting the sentence to exclude all but the most interesting parts, we obtain something like:

   Two blocks each contain 3 pulleys.

The first noun phrase 'two blocks' introduces a new entity. Because the phrase is plural, this entity is understood to have an 'external' dependency; moreover the number associated with the dependency is given as 2. Hence the initial state of the entity is something like

   entity: block1
   dep list: [(external,2,F). . .]

(where '. . .' denotes a place where more information can be added). Note that the 'usage flag' is 'false'—we cannot distinguish between the blocks along the 'external' dimension at the moment. Since this is the only dependency, the entity is unbroken. Also, there is room for more dependencies to be added—this would be necessary if the sentence were 'two blocks are attached to each table', for instance. The processing of this noun phrase will naturally result in the generation of some 'new' assertions, to state that all the objects referred to are blocks. These can be expressed wholly in terms of the 'typical element', giving something like

isa(block,block1)

There is no point in worrying about expanding this information in terms of the individual blocks—the appropriate level to express it is at the typical element (see Section 6.2.1). Indeed, it would not be possible to consider individuals if the noun phrase did not provide a number or if there were a pending quantifier.

The analysis of the second noun phrase is analogous to that of the first, and so this gives rise to an entity

entity: pulley1
dep list: [(external,3,F). . .]

and an assertion

isa(pulley,pulley1)

Now we must consider the relationship predicated between the blocks and the pulleys. There is a clear dependency here of the pulleys on the blocks—for each block there is a distinct set of pulleys. This is represented firstly as an addition to the list for 'pulley1', giving as a result

entity: pulley1
dep list: [(external,3,F),(block1,2,F). . .]

(There is still room for more depndencies.) The relationship is then further established by the creation of a *link* between the 'external' dependency of 'block1' and the 'block1' dependency of 'pulley1'. Now the meaning of the 'contain' relationship must be expanded out into assertions. Once again, it makes sense to strive for the most abstract level of processing possible. The sentence can be seen as asserting that the typical block contains the typical element of the corresponding set of pulleys. Thus an example of a new assertion that might be generated is

in(pulley1,block1)

Does this express the correct relationship? In this example, not all pulleys are in all blocks—each pulley is only in the one block that it depends on. The situation is, in fact, as follows:

In block1.1:

pulley1.1.1
pulley1.2.1
pulley1.3.1

In block1.2:

> pulley1.1.2
> pulley1.2.2
> pulley1.3.2

When we consider the meaning of'in(pulley1,block1)' the consistency restriction for linked dependencies demands that the second subscript on 'pulley1' must be the same as the first on 'block1'. Hence the assertion actually means

(X)   (Y)   in(pulley1.X.Y,block1.Y)

The restriction ensures that, for instance, 'in(pulley1.1.2,block1.2)' is true, but 'in(pulley1.3.1,block1.2)' is not. So this relatively complex proposition is expressed correctly and concisely using 'typical elements' and the dependency list representation.

4.5 A Note on Intensional Representations

At this point, we should clarify just to what extent the kinds of world model entities being proposed are 'intensional', lest there be any misunderstanding.

In the discussion of 'coextension', we remarked that it is unreasonable to expect a language understanding system ever to stop discovering correspondences between objects introduced in different contexts. Hence we are led to model the world in terms of entities embodying a certain amount of redundancy—several distinct entities may in fact correspond to the same object in the world. The reason why there is this proliferation of entities is that we have to consider each object description as potentially introducing something new. An entity 'particle1' in the world model represents, not some particular object, but an intensional concept such as 'the particle mentioned as the subject of sentence 37'. (This reference to the place of mention is analogous to the 'evoke' terms in the invoking descriptions of Webber [Webber 79].) Thus, if two model entities are found to correspond to the same object in the world, they are not collapsed into one. Rather, the 'coextension' information is recorded elsewhere, so that it can be used for making inferences.

Although the entities in our world model have an intensional nature, nevertheless they are concerned with particular, finite, sets of objects, rather than more abstract concepts. A phrase such as 'a 3 lb particle' does not give rise to an entity corresponding to the concept of '3 lb particle'—it does not express 'what it means' to be a 3 lb particle, but simply that a particular object or set of objects with these properties is being considered. Hence two identical phrases in different places give rise to different entities. However, an entity such as that arising from 'a 3 lb particle' does in some sense 'represent' the properties given in the description. This is because the only properties that this object is known to have initially are the essential properties of the '3 lb particle' concept. It follows that all inferences made about it are essentially intensional inferences about this concept, even though they are not expressed as such.

4.6   Limitations—Other Uses of Indefinite Noun Phrases

In this work, we have considered indefinite noun phrases in only a very narrow sense—where an indefinite noun phrase is used to introduce a finite number of specific objects to the hearer. A comprehensive natural-language-understanding program must be able to cope with at least the following other uses:

— To state general laws. Indefinite noun phrases can also be used when general facts or laws are being stated, as in:

   A string has two ends.

It is arguable that the meanings of such sentences must be expressed as complex logical formulae, and the simple assertions that we consider here are certainly not adequate for this. It is not clear whether the mechanisms presented here for dealing with finite quantification can be extended to cover these examples. In particular, we would need to represent the fact that membership of a set may depend on some semantic criterion (such as being a string), rather than being a simple consequence of the makeup of the dependency list.

— To indicate choice within a set. In sentences such as:

   Pick up a red block.

an indefinite noun phrase may refer to an unspecified element of a known set. This phenomenon seems to belong mainly to questions and commands, for the selection of an appropriate element is generally a task to be attempted during problem-solving (see Section 8.2.3). However, Section 8.3.3 describes some of the problems with selecting elements of sets in declarative sentences. We have not attempted to tackle these.

Our mechanisms do not work directly for these other uses of indefinite noun phrases. Nor do we present any algorithm for detecting in what way a given noun phrase is being used. Whether these gaps can be filled is a matter for further work to determine.

4.7   Summary

This chapter has considered how various partial information about the entities arising from indefinite noun phrases can be represented and manipulated. It seems that early decisions about coextension, cardinality and quantifier scope are not always essential for a deep level of semantic analysis. Much of the semantic interpretation can take place at an abstract level neutral with respect to these uncertainties, and the information generated can be interpreted at any time in the light of whatever more specific details are available. The most important idea is that of formulating assertions in terms of 'typical elements' and of using dependency lists to express information about what these stand for.

Chapter 5

DEFINITE PHRASES REFERRING TO SETS

The use of dependency lists allows us to express economically complex propositions about indefinite noun phrase entities. However, these are not the only entities in the world model—we also have the reference entities of Chapter 3, and we must consider how plural definite phrases and 'each' phrases are to be handled. In order for us to be able to deal with assertions about mixtures of different kinds of entities, there must be some compatibility between the various representations. This chapter extends the dependency list idea to cover new kinds of world model entities, so that in the end a dependency list is defined for everything in the world model.

5.1 Representing Definite Sets

This section will consider the representation of the referents of plural definite noun phrases (but not pronouns). Just as in the case of singular references, there is the possibility that the evaluation of these phrases cannot take place locally and that it may be necessary to consider various candidate referents in parallel. However, considering candidates in parallel is not as straightforward as in the singular reference case.

5.1.1 Sets with Individuals as Candidate Elements

Usually when a definite reference to a set occurs (e.g. in 'the particles'), there are a number of individuals that could be covered by the description given. It would be advantageous to keep our options open for as long as possible as to which of these are actually in the set. In many cases we might expect to be able to do this by carrying out semantic operations (performing inferences and adding to the database) at the level of the typical element of the set. Thus we might be able to avoid early over-commitment by working at an abstract level. However, there is no guarantee that semantic operations on these sets can always be performed validly at the level of the typical element. This is because there is no reason to suppose that the elements will be indistinguishable in the same way as we found with indefinite noun phrases. Hence the detailed semantic analysis of the common properties may involve different assertions being relevant to different elements. If the elements are distinguishable, the interpretation of the properties may have to be tailored to the individual peculiarities of each element (see Section 6.2.1).

The only alternative to dealing in terms of a typical element is to generate assertions in terms of the individual elements. Unfortunately, for this we must be clear what the elements are. Otherwise the database will fill up with assertions about candidates that are later rejected. For instance, if we were confronted with:

The particles are fixed.

and the known particles were {p1,p2,p3} then it would be very dangerous to add to the database

    fixed(p1).
    fixed(p2).
    fixed(p3).

until we were sure that these three entities were all being referred to by the phrase. Notice why this problem does not arise with singular references. Since with these we are certain that in the end assertions can be made about the entity as a whole (it corresponding to a single individual) we never have to phrase assertions about it in terms of candidates. So if we were processing the sentence:

The particle is fixed.

with the same particles available, we would have the option of adding

    fixed(ref(3))

(where 'ref(3)' was the reference entity involved) and keeping our options open. If different candidates were to call for different treatments in the semantic operation for 'fixed', we would force a decision so that we could still treat the reference as a single item. Such an approach would not be justified for plural references.

Because of this problem, it seems not to be feasible to keep the options for definite sets open for very long. But if this is not done, choices have to be made about the membership. Unfortunately, if there are n candidate members, there are $2^n - 1 - n$ possible (plural) sets. This would produce a large number of possibilities to consider.

A pragmatic way out of this is to suggest that such states of ignorance rarely arise in practice. Perhaps plural definite phrases are supposed to be exhaustive—that is, 'the particles' means *all* the particles (maybe restricted by some focusing criteria). If this is so, it is to be expected that the constraints provided in the noun phrase itself will be just strong enough to identify the correct set. Thus when we wish to manipulate the set after these constraints have been applied, we can do so with confidence that the correct decision has been made. We can see the representation of the set as having two stages. While constraints are still being applied, candidates can be rejected. However, as soon as we start considering 'new' information about the set, a final decision must be taken and the representation 'frozen' in its current state.

How are the constraints to be applied before a final decision is made about the set? Examples such as:

> The 3 lb particles that lie on the smooth table   (5.1)

suggest that we can use a filtering technique similar to that used for singular references. We can eliminate candidates for membership of the set just as we did then. In this example the candidate list can be filtered by the successive constraints in exactly the same way as in 'the 3 lb particle that lies on the smooth table'. The only difference is that we no longer expect just one object to satisfy the restrictions. All these similarities suggest that initially the set should be represented in the same way as a singular reference.† So it looks as if the representation as a reference entity is adequate for what happens before the set is decided on. What about the representation afterwards? After the filtering process is complete, we have found the elements that make up the set referred to. This information must be stored as qualifying knowledge about an entity that represents the set in the world model. This entity has an 'external' dependency corresponding to the set of elements that has been found; it can also never obtain more dependencies through the effects of quantification (Section 5.2). However, we cannot treat it in exactly the same way as an indefinite noun phrase entity. This is because the collection of tokens representing the sub-entities is given to us in advance, rather than being implicitly available through the mechanism of adding subscripts. So we treat such a 'set entity' as a special case, giving it a name of the form 'set(n)', where n is an integer.

To demonstrate the stages of representation a definite set entity might go through, let us consider briefly a possible sequence for the phrase in example (5.1). The computer program would start semantic processing on this phrase by considering the meaning of the noun. Thus the initial state of the entity would be the same as that of a reference entity with all the known particles as its candidates, something like

---

† However, notice that we must make an assumption that all constraints will be 'distributive' (Section 6.3.2) for this to work.

reference entity: ref(2)
candidates: {p1,p2,p3,p4}

After the rest of the phrase was processed, some candidates would have been eliminated by the constraints, leaving something like

reference entity: ref(2)
candidates: {p1,p3,p4}

This would then become 'finalised', as soon as we needed to express 'new' information about the set, to

set entity: set(1),
elements: {p1,p3,p5}
dep list: [(external,3,T)]

To summarise, assuming that a plural definite phrase has a set of candidate individuals, it goes through two stages of representation. While processing of the set continues to be in a 'given' environment it behaves as a singular reference with candidates. When it finally emerges into a 'new' environment, the remaining candidates become fixed as the elements of the set. From then on the set behaves essentially as a broken indefinite NP entity whose 'external' decomposition is given by this set of elements.

5.1.2 More Complex Candidate Sets

Unfortunately, it is naive to hope that a collection of single individuals can be obtained as the initial candidate list for a plural definite NP. The entities satisfying a given constraint are just as likely to be complex entities such as typical elements. We can eliminate some spurious possibilities by insisting that candidates not be 'broken' entities. Thus if a set of particles has been mentioned and 'broken', it is superfluous to have the typical particle as well as each of the individual particles as possible constituents of 'the particles'. However, if a candidate covering several objects is not 'broken' we may have no alternative but to treat it as some kind of compound candidate:

Some particles are free to move on a smooth table.
The particles have mass b and c.   (5.2)

Our interpretation of 'some' is as a word introducing a plural indefinite phrase with no explicit number. 'Some particles' will hence give rise to something like

entity: particle1
dep list: [(external,_,F)...]

When we see 'the particles' we must consider candidate entities that are particles. However, the only particles encountered so far are those covered by the typical element 'particle1'. It is not possible to obtain individuals as candidates unless this entity is specially broken, and this cannot be done before the size of the set is known. Even if it were possible, it would involve choosing an unnecessarily low level at which to process the set. In this case we seem to want to say that the definite phrase gives rise to an entity 'the same as' the typical element 'particle1'. However, there may not always be only one typical element candidate, and we must be prepared to handle the case when there is more than one. Moreover, since quantification rules will need to distinguish between definite and indefinite entities, the entity arising from the definite reference must be distinguishable from the original 'particle1'. We will make the assumption that if all the candidates that have been found are typical elements then only one will turn out to be correct. Given this, the appropriate representation seems to involve a generalisation of our reference entity concept. Previously we considered a reference entity to represent an individual which was one of a set of candidate individuals; what is needed here is a typical element which is one of a set of typical elements.

Thus a plural reference which has sets as candidates is appropriately represented as a kind of reference entity. How are such entities to be accommodated in our representation scheme? Since reference entities can now represent sets, we must consider giving them dependency lists (previously they always stood for individuals and could be considered to have empty dependency lists). We can define the dependency list of a reference entity to be that of its one valid candidate. Much of the work of interpreting propositions about sets cannot take place before the dependency lists of the entities involved are available. Therefore an early decision on a candidate will often be needed for entities of this kind.

The representation for the entity evoked by the definite phrase in (5.2) would be something like

> reference entity: ref(1)
> candidates: {particle1}
> dep list: [(external,_,F). . .]

where the dependency list was, in fact, that of 'particle1'.

The above paragraphs describe two ways of handling plural definite phrases, according to whether the candidates are single individuals or typical elements. It is not clear what should happen if there is a mixture of these. In such a case, the system will have to make a straight choice and be prepared to backtrack. However, it may well be that such situations arise rarely or not at all (we have not found any naturally occurring examples). The computer program takes the simplified view that the candidates left for a set entity will either be one compound entity (a typical element giving the whole set) or be a collection of simple entities (being the elements of the set). It cannot handle cases where there is a mixture of the two types (but no real examples of this have been found).

5.2 Representing 'Each' Phrases

This section considers how we can appropriately represent the referent of a phrase such as 'each particle' in our system. A traditional view of words such as 'each' is that they introduce quantifiers into the logical form of the sentence. However, as we noted in Section 1.3.3, the kinds of structured logical formulae used by people such as Woods and Colmerauer to handle quantification do not fit well into an incremental semantics framework. Such a representation scheme does not support the independent processing of separate noun phrases and allows meaning structures to be built only after global analyses of whole sentences. Webber [Webber 79] has done important work characterising what quantified noun phrases make available for subsequent anaphoric reference, but she has been concerned with unpacking a complete logical formula that has already been constructed. Our concern will be with developing a representation that can change incrementally as information is obtained from the text. Thus we will attempt to deal with quantification by performing local operations on the sets referred to by noun phrases. Given that we have adopted a dependency list representation for such sets, we must decide what the dependency list for the entity invoked by a phrase such as 'each particle' looks like. We must also decide how (if at all) the entity differs from what we get from the corresponding phrase 'the particles'. The representation that we will use will also apply to phrases such as 'each of the particles' and plural phrases followed by 'each', as in 'the particles each have . . .'.

The first thing to note about 'each' phrases is that they have many of the features of ordinary singular phrases. Thus they often appear in the same syntactic contexts as singular phrases and often allow for pronominalisation with singular pronouns. This is in accordance with the intuitive feeling that they are emphasising the idea of a set consisting of individual elements, rather than the idea of a set as a whole.

> Each particle is attached to the two strings.
> When each particle hits the wall, it rebounds . . .

The first of these sentences does not conjure up the picture of a 1–1 correspondence between particles and strings that a similar sentence with 'the particles' might. Also, the singular pronoun sounds perfectly natural in the second sentence. (Opinions differ about the applicability of a plural pronoun here.)

Secondly, an 'each' phrase communicates a set of objects–indeed, the same set that would be communicated by the corresponding plural phrase. We should thus expect the world model entity evoked to have a very similar structure of dependencies to the one that would arise from the plural phrase.

The way we have tackled the representational problems associated with 'each' phrases and their referents has been to consider that there are several ways to talk about a given set. If one uses the plural forms, certain aspects are highlighted, and if one uses the singular forms, others are highlighted instead. However, this is only really a 'surface' phenomenon—the same set is being talked about in both cases. The surface markings are important when one attempts to expand propositions about sets into propositions about individuals (Chapter 6), but they are no longer significant when one considers the deeper semantics.

Since there is only one set involved, regardless of which kind of phrase is used, we need only one entity in the world model, and this will be set up the same in both cases. Since we already have mechanisms for producing world model entities for plural definite phrases, we can use these for both. However, there must also be a way of marking a *mention* of an entity so that the surface information is not lost. So the referent of an 'each' phrase is specially marked by a '#' annotation in the computer program. This mark is purely for the sake of characterising how the entity is mentioned, and is no longer presented in any assertions that are generated. The effect of its presence is that, when the entity's dependency list is retrieved, the 'external' dependency (which will normally be present for a plural phrase) is seen under a different name.† This ensures that it will be seen not to have arisen from an ordinary plural definite phrase.

As an example of the treatment of 'each' phrases, consider the sentence:

Each particle is on a table.

The processing of the subject noun phrase goes through three phases. The first two correspond to what would happen if the phrase were 'the particles'. Assuming that there are individual candidates for the particles, we start with a reference entity

entity: ref(1)
candidates: {p1,p2,p3}

Having finished with the constraints provided by the phrase, we convert this to a set entity

set entity: set(1)
elements: {p1,p2,p3}
dep list: [(external,3,T)]

The final step is to mark the referent as coming from an 'each' phrase giving

#set(1)
dep list: [(1,3,T)]

After the other noun phrase ('a table') has been interpreted, giving entity 'table1', say, the semantic operation for 'on' needs to be invoked. However, first of all, we need to know how to interpret this relation as applied to sets of objects, rather than individuals. This is done by calling a 'semantic preprocessor'. The semantic preprocessor will be given the two referents and the name of the operation, and will invoke the operation as

---

† This is produced from the name of the entity itself. If the entity is 'set(n)' then the name 'n' is used; otherwise if it is 'ref(n)' then the name of the correct candidate is used.

necessary for combinations of the elements of the sets. It is here that the distinction between having 'set(1)' or '#set(1)' is relevant.

The next chapter describes the function of semantic preprocessors in more detail.

5.3 Summary

This chapter has shown how the referents of plural definite phrases and 'each' phrases can be represented in our framework. This concludes the development of the system of representation for noun phrase referents.

We now look at how it is possible to use this representation system to correctly interpret propositions about sets and to express quantifier scope.

Chapter 6

SEMANTIC PREPROCESSORS

English provides many ways of economically conveying large amounts of information in short phrases. In particular, a single statement about a set or several sets can expand into a large number of simpler statements about individual elements. A computer program interpreting such statements will often have to perform this expansion, even if it uses the methods of Chapter 4 to avoid considering unnecessary details. One possible method is for every semantic operation that is invoked to find the right level of detail and then to generate assertions at this level. However, there seem to be general principles about how people talk about sets which hold almost independently of the semantic operations involved, and it would be conceptually clearer to keep these distinct from the details of the semantics. In Bobrow and Webber's terms, it is sensible to separate out the *combinatoric aspects* of a sentence's interpretation. Therefore it is appropriate to consider a set of *semantic preprocessors*, one of which is invoked whenever any semantic analysis is requested. A semantic preprocessor will examine the entities that are involved in the relationship and then call the appropriate semantic operation repeatedly for all the necessary subcases. As an example, in the processing of the sentence 'the particles rest on a table', at some point the meaning of the preposition 'on' will need to be consulted. The sentence mentions a compound 'on' relationship between the particles ('particle1' and 'particle2', say) and the table ('table1', say). This can be split up into simpler relationships before semantic operations are invoked. Here it would be reasonable for the semantic preprocessor to call the 'on' operations for the pair ⟨particle1,table1⟩ and then for the pair ⟨particle2,table1⟩.

In order to find out about the entities it is concerned with, a semantic preprocessor must look at the dependency lists. While it is looking at these, it may decide that there should be a correspondence between two different dependencies, in which case it can *link* them together. It may also decide that one entity should inherit one or more dependencies from another. Thus, before semantic preprocessors can appropriately decompose a relationship involving a set of entities, they must establish how those entities are bound together. This is effectively making decisions about quantifier scope.

We will now examine some of the principles that could be embodied in semantic preprocessors. The rules that we suggest are in fact those used in the computer program. Since many semantic operations are unary or binary and others tend to decompose into operations of these types, we will confine our attention to the unary and binary cases. We will also consider only relationships with reasonable 'distributive' properties. Non-distributive properties will be discussed briefly in Section 6.3.2.

6.1   Naming and Linking Dependencies

When a semantic preprocessor looks at an entity's dependency list, the most important information actually comes from the names given to the dependencies. From these, it is possible to determine the origin of the dependencies—something which is essential for correct decisions about linking. In the previous chapters, we have encountered two situations which dependencies are created and given names.

1. A plural phrase always gives rise to an entity with an 'external' dependency—marked appropriately with the name 'external'.
2. A singular phrase usually gives rise to an entity with an empty dependency list. However, if it is an 'each' phrase, there is a dependency named after the entity itself.

We now look briefly at places where linking and copying of dependencies seem appropriate, to see how these naming conventions can be exploited.

6.1.1 'External Pairing'

When a relation between two sets is expressed with two plural noun phrases, very often the intended interpretation is as if the word 'respectively' is present. Thus the normal interpretation of 'two particles have mass b and c' is that one particle has mass b and the other mass c—the elements of the two sets are 'paired' together. A semantic preprocessor might well benefit from a rule that recognised this situation, which we might call 'external pairing'. For the kinds of semantic operations involved in mechanics problems, this would produce reasonable results. The main doubts that arise follow from the fact that the interpretation taken is in no sense a *logical* consequence of the way the sentence is formulated. For instance, in 'the particles are attached to the strings', theoretically particles could be associated with strings in many possible ways. In practice, people wishing to communicate do not seem to use such vague phrasing unless there are clear conventions. The only other reasonable possibility for this example has all combinations of particles and strings attached to one another. This can be much more clearly formulated as either:

Each particle is attached to the strings.

or:

The particles are attached to each string.

(Note that, because the 'each' phrases are singular, the rule no longer applies here.)

Partial semantic evidence can be found for our interpretation in many examples where the relationship has uniqueness properties. Thus, for instance, in 'the particles are on the tables' it is clearly impossible for any one particle to be on more than one table. However, semantics cannot provide a general solution for ambiguities of this type.

How can a semantic preprocessor make use of this rule? In terms of dependency lists, all we have said is that if both entities have an 'external' dependency then the semantic operation must be invoked for pairs of sub-entities that correspond along this dimension. So if the two entities are

entity: e1   dep list: [(external,2,F). . .]
entity: e2   dep list: [(external,2,T). . .]

then we should only consider calling the operation with arguments

(e1.1, e2.1)
(e1.2, e2.2)

This correspondence between the two 'external' dependencies can be expressed by *linking* the dependencies together in the way we considered in Section 4.4.3. A binary semantic preprocessor that incorporates this kind of pairing between sets can therefore use the rule that two dependencies named 'external' should always be linked. In fact, for the examples we will consider, we can state that for a binary operation *any* two dependencies with the same name should be linked. This will turn out to help us with examples involving quantification.

6.1.2 'Each' Quantification

The consideration of 'each' phrases naturally brings up the problem of representing quantifier scope in the semantic analysis. Quantifier scope is normally seen as an aspect of the global structure of a sentence, so that it cannot be completely determined or expressed until the whole of the input has been examined. Our framework of early, local semantic interpretation does not allow this view because it does not fit in with the idea of building meaning representations incrementally. Instead we view quantifier scope as a way of expressing dependencies between sets, and attempt to determine these locally during semantic preprocessing.

When the effect of universal quantification is examined, it is apparent that the distinction between definite and indefinite phrases is important. Thus:

> Each rod is on the table   (6.1)

has quite a different structure to:

> Each rod is on a table   (6.2)

In the first of these, the relative scope of 'the' and 'each' is irrelevant. Neither phrase depends on the other, and the processing of the relationship is adequately covered by our previous rules. In the second case there is possible ambiguity about the relative scope of 'each' and 'a'. This creates the possibility that the table entity depends on the set of rods (the definite determiner 'shields' the table from this in (6.1)). Because of this difference, in the preprocessing of semantic operations there must be a rule looking out for the combination of a universally quantified phrase with an indefinite phrase. Which decision should be made about the relative scopes? In the examples that we have found, the reading with the 'universal' quantifier dominating the 'existential' has usually seemed to be the preferred interpretation. There are two reasons for picking this reading:

— If the alternative is meant, it is usually more clearly stated using a device to make the existential phrase definite, for instance:

> There is a table and each rod is on it   (6.3)

— This reading makes fewer assumptions about the scene described. That is, since (6.3) implies our preferred reading of (6.2), the latter is always correct, even if it is incomplete. If it is later discovered that all the tables are the same, it is conceivable that this could be dealt with as extra information (in the spirit of Section 4.1).

Given this preferred reading for the combination of universal and existential quantifiers, how is it to be reflected in the way semantic operations are performed? Firstly, since the indefinite entity is to depend on the set, all the dependencies that the set has should be copied into its dependency list. Secondly, these dependencies should be linked to their copies, so that we only consider 'corresponding elements' in the relationship. During the copying, we need only create a new dependency if the indefinite entity does not already have one of the same name. This avoids the possible situation where one entity depends on another several times.

Let us now consider the stages of analysis for example (6.2), firstly when the set of rods is known by its elements. The initial set of rods is represented by something like

> set entity: set(1), elements: {r1,r2,r3}
> dep list: [(external,3,T)]

and the derived '#set(1)' with

> dep list: [(1,3,T)]

represents the referent of 'each rod'. Notice that '#set(1)' is distinguished from 'set(1)' by having the 'external' dependency seen under the name of the entity itself. The referent of 'a table' is something like

entity: table1   dep list: [. . .]

According to the rule, when the 'on' relation is considered, the semantic preprocessor should copy all the dependencies of '#set(1)' across to 'table1', linking the corresponding entries. This results in the following situation:

entity: set(1)   dep list: [(external,3,T)]
                                    >—These dependencies linked
entity: table1   dep list: [(1,3,T). . .]

We can then generate assertions such as

on(r1,table1.1)   on(r2,table1.2)   on(r3,table1.3)

   In this case the set quantified over is given by a special 'set' entity (see Section 5.1), which has one dependency. This dependency is 'copied' across to the depending entity. If sentence (6.1) were preceded by something like 'A room contains some rods of length 2l', with the rods represented by an unbroken entity

entity: rod1
dep list: [(external,_,F). . .]

the results would look more like the following. The reference to the set of rods would give rise to a reference entity with the same dependency list as 'rod1':

reference entity: ref(1), referring to rod1
dep list: [(external,_,F). . .]

The derived '#ref(1)' with

dep list: [(rod1,_,F). . .]

would be the referent of the phrase 'each rod'. Notice again that '#ref(1)' is distinguished from 'ref(1)' is how the 'external' dependency is seen. The referent of 'a table' would again be

entity: table1   dep list: [. . .]

After the 'on' relation has been processed, the entities would look like

entity: rod1   dep list: [(external,_,F). . .]
                                    >—These dependencies linked
entity: table1   dep list: [(rod1,_,F). . .]

We would then be able to generate an assertion such as

on(rod1,table1)

Thus, for these simple cases the effects of quantifier scope can be achieved by the appropriate matching operations on dependency lists together with the existing conventions for interpreting underspecified assertions.

6.1.3 Sharing Information by Linking

When two dependencies of entities involved in a binary relation are linked, valuable new information about the objects can be obtained. Since we interpret a link between dependencies as implying a 1–1 correspondence along that dimension, the two numbers associated with the dependencies must be equal. Thus if one is known but the other is not, the value can be simply copied across. Similarly if the usage flag for one entity is 'T' then this value must also be taken by the other flag. The 'T' value means that the sub-entities along the dimension we are considering are distinguishable. The semantic operation will be generating assertions in terms of corresponding elements, and so the sub-entities of the other entity will be distinguishable through their appearance in these assertions. For example, consider the two entities

   entity: e1 dep list: [(external,2,F). . .]
   entity: e2 dep list: [(external,2,T). . .]

'e1's dependency is marked 'F', which means that up to now all operations on this entity have been expressed in terms of the typical element. So at this point the sub-entities 'e1.1' and 'e.1.2' are not distinguishable. On the other hand, 'e2's dependency is marked 'T', and so at some point the sub-entities 'e2.1' and 'e2.2' must have been treated differently. If some binary relationship, for instance 'contact', is predicated between these entities, the semantic preprocessor will recognise 'external pairing' and link the two dependencies together. When the semantic operation is invoked, it will generate assertions such as

   contact(e1.1,e2.1)
   contact(e1.2,e2.2)

Once this has been done, e1.1 and e1.2 are suddenly distinguishable. So the 'F' flag must be changed to 'T'; this can be done in the preprocessing. Even when nothing new is contributed directly by a link between dependencies, it is still useful to bind together the corresponding components, so that further information about one leads immediately to more knowledge about the other.

  The following example (from [McKenzie 60]) illustrates how cardinality information can propagate by means of this stage of semantic preprocessing.

   Two gear wheels . . . are mounted on
   frictionless spindles.   (6.4)

Here the number of spindles is not communicated directly by the noun phrase but can be deduced as a result of the pairing between wheels and spindles. Before the 'mounted on' relation is processed, the spindles entity has an unknown number associated with its 'external' dependency. When the relation is processed, this information is 'shared' with the 'external' information of the wheels. Hence the number 2 is communicated across (and the dependency will be 'used' if and only if that of the wheels entity is). Assuming that the gear wheels are represented as an unbroken entity (at the stage we are concerned with), the two entities before the 'mounted on' operation appear as

    entity: wheel1   dep list: [(external,2,F). . .]
    entity: spindle1   dep list: [(external,_,F). . .]

After the pairing, the latter looks like

    entity: spindle1   dep list: [(external,2,F). . .]

and assertions such as the following are in the database:

    mountedon(wheel1,spindle1)

The meaning of this assertion expresses the correct pairing behaviour because of the conventions of interpretation given in Section 4.4.

6.2   Decomposing Complex Relationships

6.2.1   Unary Operations on Complex Entities

When we have to process a relationship involving a complex entity, we may not always be justified in picking the most abstract level possible for carrying out the semantic operation. Some operations on sets cannot be reliably phrased in terms of typical elements, but rely on the availability of individual elements for their expression. Consider the following excerpt from a problem concerning a V-shaped groove (from [Street 29]):

    . . . the faces of the groove each making angles beta
    with the vertical plane . . .   (6.5)

Here there is a single modifier ('making angles beta with . . .') applied to a compound entity ('the faces'). The modifier is even 'distributive', inasmuch as it is true for each face that it 'makes angle beta with . . .'. However, things are not so simple. Although the modulus of both of the angles is beta, the two angles have different senses (otherwise the faces would be parallel). Thus, although it is possible to express some of the information given by this phrase at the level of the typical face (i.e. the modulus of the angle), the fact that we know that the faces are different means that some information (i.e. the sense of the angle) must be expressed separately for each individual.

This situation is likely to arise frequently in a system carrying out a deep level of semantic analysis. In such a system, a (linguistically) simple statement can expand into a large set of predictions, expressing the fine details of the situation. For instance, a simple statement that 'A is in equilibrium' might give rise to a large number of assertions, expressing which parts of A are in what positions, what values various parameters of A have and so on. The assertions for 'being in equilibrium' are likely to be different for each object the description is applied to. Thus, if this modifier is applied to a set it is unlikely that assertions can be produced at the level of the typical element. Instead, the manipulations must be carried out for each individual, with assertions produced which are tailored to its own peculiarities and appropriateness judged in terms of its own particular situation.

How can one decide at what level to decompose the work involved in unary operations on indefinite NPs? One principle is clear:

1. Applying an operation to an 'unbroken' entity need not involve considering sub-entities.

The validity of this principle follows from the fact that an 'unbroken' entity represents a homogeneous mass of objects (as far as we currently know), which behave identically under inference. Otherwise the differences between elements would have required making a proper 'break' along one dimension of the entity. All checks and assertions about 'unbroken' entities can be made 'in one go'. The example of the blocks of pulleys in Chapter 4 illustrates this happening. At no stage in the problem does any of the entities become 'broken'. Hence it is never necessary to consider individual objects.

It is obviously most efficient to do all semantic processing at the highest (most abstract) level possible. However, what happens when an entity has been 'broken'? Whether the operation can be carried out at the highest level now depends on whether the processing in the operation makes use of properties that are held by some of, but not all, the elements of the set. If it does, different elements may satisfy semantic checks in different ways or assertions of different forms may have to be generated for different elements. In this case it is essential to consider each of the sub-entities individually. Example (6.5) illustrates this. The set of faces is 'broken' because the representation of a groove involves a way of distinguishing between the faces. The semantic operation for 'making an angle beta with . . .' must produce different assertions for each face, and this is betrayed by the 'brokenness' of the faces entity.

Since it is hard to tell in advance whether a semantic operation makes use of properties that elements of a set disagree on, there are two possible strategies for handling 'broken' entities. Firstly, one can attempt to do the processing at the highest possible level and resort to lower levels if this fails. Secondly, one can always do the processing at the lowest level where the entities are distinguishable. The latter is the approach taken in the computer program. That is, we take the lowest level where the entities are already broken and perform the operation at that level. In either case, the following principle holds:

1. In general, most operations on a 'broken' entity must consider all the sub-entities individually.

So far in this discussion we have only considered situations where the entity involved has one dependency. If a unary operation is applied to a more complex entity, it is necessary to consider each dimension separately, using the principles we have obtained. Thus, for example, an operation on

> entity: p
> dep list: [(a,2,T),(b,_,F),(c,3,T). . .]

must in general consider individually the entities

> p.1.X.1   p.1.X.2   p.1.X.3
> p.2.X.1   p.2.X.2   p.2.X.3

for variable X.

6.2.2 Binary Operations

The basic principles for decomposing unary relations according to the brokenness of the entities can also be used for binary relations. We just need to consider each entity separately, picking an appropriate level of abstraction using our criteria. The basic semantic operation can then be invoked for all possible pairs of sub-entities, one from each of the arguments. The only restriction is that we must always choose consistent values along dependencies that are linked. Thus the assumption is that all restrictions on valid pairs will have been expressed in advance through dependency linking.

As a simple example, a binary relationship between the entities

> entity: e1   dep list: [(a,2,T),(b,_,F). . .]
>
> These dependencies linked
>
> entity: e2   dep list: [(b,_,F),(c,2,T). . .]

(where the two 'b' dependencies are linked) would decompose by our rules into relationships between the following pairs:

> ⟨e1.1.X,e2.X.1⟩
> ⟨e1.1.X,e2.X.2⟩
> ⟨e1.2.X,e2.X.1⟩
> ⟨e1.2.X,e2.X.2⟩

where X is a variable.

6.3 Limitations

6.3.1 Restrictions on Communicating Dependencies

A possible problem with communicating dependencies only when two entities participate in a semantic operation (and not using any syntactic cues) is that dependencies may exist between entities that are only indirectly related. For instance, in:

A string hanging over a pulley is placed in each lift   (6.6)

(where the desired dependencies are marked) the relationships that are
likely to be examined are that between the strings and the pulleys and that
between the lifts and the strings (if we ignore any deeper semantic manipulations). Since new dependencies are only established in the preprocessing
of semantic operations, it is not clear how the pulleys can be made dependent on the lifts (or how it can be ascertained that there is more than one
pulley). Moreover, even if this can be achieved, it is necessary to obtain the
required 'pairing' between strings and pulleys in the 'hanging over' relationships after these have been dealt with.

The solution to these problems might be to have a special way of dealing
with binary relationships involving two indefinite NP entities. When such a
relationship occurs, the two entities could be made to share the same
dependency list (apart from possible 'external' dependencies). If this is
done, the discovery of an extra dependency for one entity later on will be
immediately reflected in the dependency list of the other. Thus in the
example, the strings and pulleys would share a single dependency list after
the 'hanging over' relationship was processed. When the 'placed in' relation was dealt with, an extra entry would be made on the list for the strings.
This would be immediately reflected in that for the pulleys. How would
pairing between strings and pulleys be achieved? This would be simply a
consequence of the shared dependency and the conventions for interpreting 'underspecified' assertions (Section 4.4).

Unfortunately, such a solution would require some refinement to take
account of examples such as the following (from [Dull, Metcalfe and Williams 64]):

A bridge . . . is supported by a pier at each end   (6.7)

Here two indefinite entities (the bridge and the piers) participate in a
semantic relationship (support) but do not share all dependencies (the
dependency on the ends). The computer program can currently deal with
this example, because it has not been modified to deal with examples such
as (6.6).

6.3.2 *Problems with Non-distributive Relations*
We have used the term 'distributive' to refer to a property or relation
which, when applied to a set of objects, says the same thing about each one.
Thus 'the blocks are blue' means that each block individually is blue, for
example ('being blue' is distributive). It is unfortunately the case that we
have relied heavily on distributivity in formulating our rules for semantic
preprocessors, and in other places are well.

One place where we depend on distributivity to a large extent is in the treatment of constraints as means of reducing candidate sets. Since filtering requires considering one candidate at a time, it is only possible to do this if all the restrictions can be seen as simple constraints on single elements. An example such as:

The particles 3 ft apart   (6.8)

cannot be accommodated in this framework (we cannot go through the candidates one by one, eliminating those that are not '3 ft apart'). This example is contrived and sounds odd. Perhaps such restrictions are rarely used in practice.

Even when we consider 'new' information, it is clear that our methods will not work with properties that cannot be applied individually to all the elements of a set. Example such as:

Two spherical balls whose masses are in the ratio 3:1
are suspended side by side so that their centres are in a
horizontal line and the balls hang just touching.   (6.9)

(from [McKenzie 60]) require some 'breaking up' of the set before they can be processed and have idiosyncratic properties. These are examples of properties applied to sets as a whole rather than to individual elements (although they expand in terms of differing properties of elements).

How can we deal with non-distributive relations? There is, perhaps, no way of avoiding considering each one as a special case and specifying how it deals with sets and can use the dependency information associated with its arguments. Each non-distributive property has its own peculiar way of assigning properties to individual elements, and it is not clear what general-isations there are.

Even if we ignore the problem of blatantly non-distributive relations, we must still be aware of the problems that are introduced by the use of a uniform set of semantic preprocessors. There is a significant danger that the conceptual clarity that these offer can be achieved only at the expense of severely limiting the scope of the semantic operations. Thus, for instance, although 'a string is attached to two blocks' does indeed mean that the string is attached to the first block and the string is attached to the second block, the processing of the relationship should almost certainly see the situation as a whole. Given the global picture, a semantic routine can suggest one block being at each end of the string. Given separately the two relationships between individuals, it is much harder to decide this. It is clear that, in general, decomposing statements about sets is non-trivial, and a much more flexible system is needed that we have presented here. It might well be the case that there are very few relations that are truly 'distributive', in which case a lot more work needs to be done before we have developed a firm framework for dealing with propositions about sets.

6.4 Summary

In this chapter, we have discussed how one can build general procedures for dealing with propositions about sets. A semantic preprocessor is a procedure that decomposes complex propositions about sets into propositions about simpler objects (usually individuals). We have seen how semantic preprocessors can use the dependency list representations to organise semantic operations on sets and to achieve the effects of quantifier scope. The operation of semantic preprocessors has been seen to involve two phases—first, the appropriate copying and linking together of dependencies of the entities involved, and second the decomposition of the relationship into simpler ones, according to the 'brokenness' of the entities. Examples of the rules that one might use in these phases have been presented.

In summary, there are two main ways in which we differ from Woods and Colmerauer in our treatment of quantification:

1. Quantification scope is expressed not as the differing placement of sub-formulae within a logical formula, but as relationships ('links') between complex entities in the world model. These relationships are permanent ties between the entities and are used in the interpretation of assertions made about them.
2. The effects of quantifier scope are communicated solely through the processing of semantic relationships between entities and not as part of a global construction for the sentence.

The basis for the whole mechanism is the dependency list representation, which is similar to the representation of objects as Skolem functions, suitably modified to allow partial information to be recorded.

At the level of concrete rules for determining quantifier scope, our system produces only a small offering—that the quantification of an 'each' phrase dominates that of an indefinite phrase that it is semantically related to. This compares with the many rules used by Woods and Colmerauer, covering a variety of quantifiers as well as negation. Vanlehn's [Vanlehn 78] survey of rules for interpreting quantification in natural language shows that almost all have counter-examples (although the combination of 'each' and 'a' is fairly reliable interpreted in the way we have chosen). There are still many unsolved problems in this area.

The rules that have been informally developed for the formation of dependency lists and for the workings of semantic preprocessors can now be summarised more formally in Appendix II.

Now that the development of the representational system is complete, we look briefly at what implications it has for the inference system that is used. Then we consider the scope of our methods by looking at examples and possible extensions.

Chapter 7

THE INFERENCE SYSTEM

7.1 The Role of the Inference System

The use of a flexible system of representation for noun phrase interpretation necessarily places a burden on the inference system. Because of the intensional nature of our world model entities, there are usually more of them than there are objects in the 'world' under consideration. A fact about a single object in the world may be expressed in many possible ways according to which entities are used to represent it. Somehow sense must be made of all this information. To help it with this, the inference system must use the extra information about how typical elements of sets relate to particular elements and which entities are known to correspond to the same object in the world, as well as ordinary inference rules and the assertions in the database. The use of this extra information for our representation system can be seen as taking the form of two special inference rules.

It is worth while referring back to Fig. 2.1 to see what the role of the inference system is in our framework. We are not pretending that this is the only role that inference can play in natural language understanding, but rather we are concentrating on the aspects that most concern out work on early noun phrase interpretation. When, in our framework, a piece of semantic analysis is requested by the syntactic routines, a semantic preprocessor steps in to make multiple calls to a semantic operation. Because of this intermediate stage, the semantic operation only has to deal with 'unbroken' entities—usually entities that correspond to single objects. In the course of the analysis it performs, assertions are generated about these entities. Some of the assertions are constraints that must be satisfied—these are sent to the constraint satisfaction routines, which try substituting candidates for reference entities. It is only at this stage that the inference system is invoked—it is used in an attempt to prove the truth of an assertion expressed entirely in terms of 'unbroken' entities and in which candidates have been substituted for reference entities. Note that the context also means that all inference is goal-directed—the inference system is always presented with a specific goal to be proved. It is hence based around a simple backwards chaining approach, where a goal can be proved either if it is in the database or if there is an inference rule that can replace it by subgoals that are themselves provable.

7.2   The 'Reference' Rule

The 'reference' rule allows account to be taken of which entities in the world model could correspond to the same object in the world. A reference entity and one of its candidates are related in this way, as are two entities whose coextension has been explicitly stated (Section 4.1). The rule which enables this information to be used states that:

> If an assertion holds of one entity then it also holds of
> any other entity that could be coextensive with it.

The main use of this is to enable assertions made about reference entities to be interpreted in terms of their possible candidates. For instance, if 'ref(1)' has candidates 'a' and 'b' and 'p(ref(1))' is provable, then both 'p(a)' and 'p(b)' will be provable.

In the computer program, an explicit record is kept of pairs of entities that could be coextensive, in a way that generalises the use of candidate sets for reference entities. Thus, given an assertion to be inferred, the system can easily produce other assertions as 'equivalent' goals by substituting coextensive entities for some of the arguments.

Given this rule of inference, it is possible to deduce false propositions when a reference has more than one candidate. As an example, consider the following sequence:

> A particle slides down the side of a wedge.
> It has a mass of 5 lbs.

The phrase 'it' can be taken as referring to either the particle or the wedge, and the second sentence gives 'new' information about whichever this is. This produces an assertion such as:

> mass(ref(1),5,lbs)

where

> ref(1) one of {particle1,wedge1}

Our rule of inference enables both of

> mass(particle1,5,lbs)
> mass(wedge1,5,lbs)

to be deduced as possible consequences of this, although only one is correct (but which?). As a result, in the following analysis a constraint that the particle have non-zero mass would be satisfiable, as would a constraint that the wedge have non-zero mass. In situations such as this, the inference system will allow some constraints to be satisfied when they should not be. This is a necessary consequence of postponing reference evaluation decisions (but the problem will be much worse in a system that postpones reference evaluation completely). Fortunately, any disadvantages are on the side of the system being over-conservative and allowing too many constraints to hold. This simply gives rise to a larger search space of possible analysis paths than necessary and can never lead to the correct path being lost. In the above example, the result is that possibilities requiring either of the assertions to be true can be followed after this point. If one of the consequences were not deducible than any line of analysis that relied on it could never be tried and the search tree would be incomplete.

How efficient is it to use the 'reference' rule? If there are no reference entities around that are associated with the entities in a goal assertion, it produces very little overhead (no 'equivalent' assertions are generated). However, if there are relevant reference entities, the effect on the amount of time spent on proofs can be considerable. In our computer program, whenever there is an assertion to be proved, the alternative 'equivalent' goals are tried one by one until one succeeds. Since this applies to every subgoal generated in the proof, the presence of reference entities could cause a huge increase in the size of the search tree for a proof. In the examples we have tried, this has not been a problem, but it remains to be seen what the effect of using the 'refernce' rule will be in other situations.

The computer program is actually able to use an improved version of the 'reference' rule, at the expense of only dealing properly with reference entities (and not instances of coextension in general). This relies on the fact that the creation of reference entities always extends the set of entities in the direction of 'greater abstractness'. A new reference entity has only 'less abstract' entities as its candidates. As was remarked in the first section of this chapter, reference entities do not appear in the original goals presented to the inference system. These goals are expressed entirely in terms of 'least abstract' entities. Now, if a fact has been put in the database about one of these 'least abstract' entities then either it appears in terms of the entity itself or it appears in terms of a more abstract entity (a reference entity which has it as a candidate). It is only necessary to produce 'equivalent' assertions that are more abstract. If one of these more abstract goals is being pursued, it is again only necessary to consider 'equivalent' goals that are even more abstract. Moreover the same applies in more lengthy inferences. For instance, if we had the goal

    fixed(particle1)

and 'particle1' was a candidate for both 'ref(1)' and 'ref(2)' then we could generate three possible 'equivalent' goals:

1. fixed(particle1)
2. fixed(ref(1))
3. fixed(ref(2))

If we also had available an inference rule

    <u>if</u> contact(A,B) <u>and</u> fixed(B) <u>then</u> fixed(A)

and decided to use it, possibility (1) would lead us to the subgoals

    contact(particle1,B) and fixed(B)

the first of which would generate two 'equivalent' goals as before. On the other hand, following possibility (2) would give us the subgoals

    contact(ref(1),B) and fixed(B)

We would not want to start generating equivalent goals to these in terms of 'particle1', because this would duplicate the investigations going on for possibility (1). This would be avoided if we used the 'abstractness' criterion, because 'ref(1)' is more 'abstract' than 'particle1'. The situation is perhaps best expressed pictorially, with each reference entity placed above its candidates (Fig. 7.1).

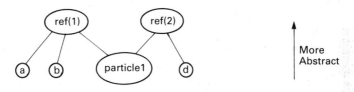

Fig. 7.1 – Typical layout of reference entities

In this scheme, new reference entities are added at the top of the diagram, whereas new indefinite entities are added at the bottom. If a fact has been stated about 'a' in this example, it has been explicitly stated either in terms of 'a' or in terms of 'ref(1)' (or a mixture of the two). If a fact has been stated about 'ref(1)' then it cannot have been stated in terms of any other entity. Goals given to the inference system are always in terms of entities at the bottom of the diagram, and so it is only necessary to follow links 'upwards' to generate equivalent subgoals. In particular, inferences such as 'p(a) implies p(ref(1)) implies p(b)' are not desirable, and can be avoided.

7.3 The 'Compound Entity' Rule

The 'compound entity' rule enables the relationship between typical elements of sets and particular elements to be taken into account. It is used to infer particular consequences from general assertions about sets, and embodies the conventions for interpreting 'underspecified' assertions (Section 4.4). The rule is only necessary for interpreting information about those sets that arise from indefinite noun phrases—all information about definite 'set entities' (5.1) is necessarily immediately expressed in terms of individual elements (because such entities are 'broken'). The rule states that:

> If an assertion containing one or more 'underspecified' indefinite entities holds, then a derived assertion obtained by adding 'subscripts' to the entities holds as long as:

1. Subscripts occur in an order that corresponds to the order of dependencies in the dependency lists, with no 'gaps'.
2. Each subscript is a legal value for the dependency it corresponds to.
3. Any two added subscripts that correspond to linked dependencies must be equal

The first of these restrictions is just to ensure consistency in the meaning of names with subscripts. Thus if 'particle1' has two dependencies then 'particle1.3' always refers to the typical element of the set obtained by choosing the third division of the first dependency. The corresponding typical element for the second dependency would be 'particle1.X.3', where X is a variable. The second restriction ensures that the 'number' and 'usage' information for dependencies is taken into account. If a dependency is 'unused', the only legal subscript is a variable (there is no point in considering the sub-entities along this dimension, even if we know how many there are). On the other hand, if it is 'used' then the subscript could be either a variable or an integer between 1 and the 'number'. Finally, the third restriction ensures that 'linking' information is used correctly for decoding statements about 'corresponding' elements of sets.

How is this inference rule used by the computer program? The rule is a way of deducing things about entities whose names include subscripts. Given an assertion containing such an entity, it can be used to generate subsuming assertions that may be true. Hence it is used for suggesting alternative levels at which the proof of a subgoal can proceed. If a name with a subscript occurs in a goal, a possibility is to try to prove the same goal with the subscript removed. The third restriction on the 'compound entity' rule provides a check that the new goal really does imply the old one.

As a simple example, if we have

> entity: particle1
> dep list: [(external,2,T). . .]

and the assertion

> isa(particle,particle1)

in the database, then the goal 'isa(particle,particle1.1)' will be provable by means of the 'compound entity' rule—the property of being a particle is true of an element because it is true of the typical element.

Is the inference rule presented here adequate for all inferences about sets? It enables propositions about elements to be deduced from propositions about typical elements, but gives no help for inferences in the other direction. Fortunately, as we noted in the first section of this chapter, the inference system is only called upon to satisfy goals containing 'unbroken' entities. A proposition about such an entity can only be true by dint of being expressed in terms of that entity or more 'abstract' entities (entities that represent sets including all the objects corresponding to the entity). For if an entity is 'unbroken' no semantic operations have been carried out on individual sub-entities. Thus we have a situation analogous to that with the 'reference' rule—inferences only need to consider more 'abstract' alternative goals. Hence the rule given is adequate.

How efficient is it to use the 'compound entity' rule? As in the case of the 'reference' rule, it causes an extra level of search to take place for each subgoal of a proof. The explosive nature of this search is limited somewhat by the fact that only 'more abstract' goals are proposed by it at any time. Moreover, the applicability of the rule can be detected quickly by syntactic means—a subscripted name is related syntactically to the names of the sets it is subsumed by.

7.4 General Proof Strategy

The strategy used by the computer program for attempting proofs involves mixing together the two inference rules into a single mechanism for proposing alternative goals.

Whenever a subgoal is generated, it and alternative 'more abstract' goals are proposed one by one until one can be satisfied. In order to satisfy such a goal, the system tries first to find a matching assertion in the database; failing this, it tries to find an ordinary inference rule that matches the goal and uses this to generate a new set of subgoals.

7.5 Problems with Negation

It seems reasonable to expect semantic operations to generate constraints about what must *not* be true, as well as what must be true. Hence we must examine the status of negation in the inference system, and in particular, how negation interacts with our new inference rules. Our basic strategy is to equate negation with unprovability. However, this introduces some interesting problems.

The first problem arises with the 'reference' rule, which as we remarked can prove false propositions. If the system can prove a proposition 'P' by using the 'reference' rule with a false candidate for a reference entity then it will never be able to prove 'not(P)'. For in order to establish 'not(P)' it must have completely failed to prove 'P'. This is a serious problem, because it can lead to a correct path being eliminated from the search tree.

A possible solution would be for the system to have two modes of inference—'optimistic' and 'pessimistic'. In 'optimistic' mode it would prove everything that could 'possibly' be true. This would be equivalent to the system as described, and would be the normal approach for satisfying constraints. In 'pessimistic' mode it would only prove things guaranteed to be true. Thus it would only use the 'reference' rule in situations where 'identity' was positively established. In order to produce an 'optimistic' proof of 'not(P)', the system would attempt a 'pessimistic' proof of 'P' and succeed if and only if that failed. This would guarantee that true propositions could always be proved. It would also lead to a few more false propositions being provable. The extension of the computer program to allow these two modes of inference should be straightforward, but it has not yet been undertaken.

The second problem with negation concerns the generation of subsuming alternatives for subgoals. If proposition 'P' subsumes proposition 'Q' then 'not(P)' does not (necessarily) subsume 'not(Q)'. For instance, trying to prove 'p(particle1)' is a reasonable way of proving 'p(particle1.1)', but it would be wrong to try to prove 'not(p(particle1))' in order to get 'not(p(particle1.1))'. (One cannot assume that a goal is unprovable because a more general goal is.) Our syntactic mechanism for generating alternative goals by the 'compund entity' rule does not work for negations. The action of this rule must be switched off in such contexts. It must also be possible to prevent any subgoal from being proved in a way that uses an 'over general' negation. The current program incorporates a way of doing this.

7.6   Summary

This chapter has investigated the kind of inference system that is needed to support the representation system we have developed. Two special inference rules have been described, which allow the system to make use of the extra level of information kept about world model entities.

It is now time to summarise the scope and limitations of the system as a whole.

Chapter 8

SUMMARY AND EXAMPLES

This chapter surveys a set of examples that indicate the scope of our representational system. We look firstly at examples that the computer program can deal with. Then we look at examples whose treatment seems to be within the scope of the system but which cannot at the moment be handled by it. Finally we consider examples that seem to demand more sophisticated treatment.

8.1 Capabilities of the Program

The following examples can all be processed by the computer program, and illustrate the kinds of problems that our theoretical ideas address. Many of them also appear in Appendix VI together with traces of their analysis by the program.

8.1.1 Reference Evaluation

The system of incremental reference evaluation allows the determination of the referents of definite phrases to be distributed throughout the analysis. Thus it is possible to keep on doing semantic interpretation in positions where references cannot be uniquely identified without the program being forced into early choices.

> Two pulleys of weights 12 lb and 8 lb are connected
> by a string passing over a fixed pulley.
> Over the pulley of weight 8 lbs is hung another string.
> What is the acceleration of the string which hangs
> over the fixed pulley? (8.1)

This example presents a typical mechanics problem, with definite and indefinite noun phrases occurring in various places. It serves to illustrate the symmetry between the treatments of 'given' and 'new' information. The property of having weight 8 lb is supplied in the first sentence as 'new' information about a 'new' object and in the second sentence as a constraint on a reference to be evaluated. The same applies to the property of hanging over a fixed pulley in the first and third sentences. In the program these pairs are handled almost identically, the only difference being in the generation of 'given' rather than 'new' assertions and the use of reference entities rather than indefinite entities. The filtering of candidate sets proceeds in the background without interrupting the smooth progress of the semantic analysis.

> A uniform rod is supported by a string
> attached to its ends. (8.2)

This example illustrates how the constraint propagation methods used enable semantic checks imposed in one part of the analysis to affect reference evaluation carried out in another (see Section 3.5).

8.1.2 Operations on Sets

The program is able to represent various kinds of finite sets and to expand certain kinds of propositions about sets into propositions about individual elements. It allows some flexibility for incorporating rules of various kinds for this. The rules discussed cover examples such as:

> Two particles are attached to
> the left end of a string. (8.3)

> Particles of mass b and c are attached
> to the ends of a rod. (8.4)

In the former, the program assumes that each particle is attached to the end; in the latter, it assumes a pairing between particles and ends.

It is possible to carry out semantic operations on sets before their cardinality is known.[†] The system can often continue with semantic interpretation in spite of uncertainty of this kind by dealing at the level of typical elements, to cover examples such as:

> A man holds some uniform balls. (8.5)

Moreover, the rules for handling propositions about sets enable the cardinality of some sets to be determined retrospectively, as in:

> Blocks of mass m are attached at the ends of a light rod. (8.6)

where it is concluded that there are two blocks (see Section 6.1.3).

---

† Or if the cardinality is unmanageable, as in '30000 balls'.

8.1.3 *Plural Definite Phrases*

The system can represent and cope with two types of subsequent reference to sets—where the individual members of sets are available as candidates and where only the 'typical elements' of sets are available. In the former case, it is necessary to make a 'maximality assumption'—that a plural definite noun phrase refers to the maximal set of objects that satisfy the constraints it supplies. In the latter case it is necessary to choose a candidate before any semantic operations on the set can take place. Cases with mixed candidate sets cannot be dealt with.

A situation where individual members of the set can be found is given in:

> A table supports two balls of mass 5 and 6 lbs.
> The balls are uniform.   (8.7)

A situation where only typical elements can be used is given in:

> A man holds some uniform balls.
> The balls weigh 5 lbs.   (8.8)

8.1.4 *'Each' Phrases*

The system can represent the meaning of 'each' phrases of two possible kinds, corresponding to the two different kinds of plural reference. An example of an 'each' phrase where the individual elements of the set are not available (semantic routines have not carried out any operations at that level) is:

> Two men are standing on a scaffold.
> Each man supports a uniform pole.   (8.9)

This example also shows the effect of the 'each' quantifier on indefinite phrases. The system is able to achieve the effects of quantifier scope when the objects referred to by these phrases are in a semantic relation. In this example, the program is able to tell that there are two poles and each man is supporting precisely one of them.

The program can also deal successfully with the interaction of these quantifiers when the indefinite phrase occurs first, as in:

> A bridge 60 ft long is supported by a pier at each end.   (8.10)

(from [Dull, Metcalfe and Williams 64]). The discovery that what initially appears to be a single pier is in fact two does not force any backtracking or reworking of pieces of analysis by the program. This is because the interpretation of indefinite phrases is carried out at such a level of abstractness that it remains valid even when extra information of this kind appears. The system does not have to make early decisions about indefinite phrases, but can proceed smoothly with an incremental interpretation.

The interaction of sets and quantifiers can be handled smoothly, allowing examples such as:

> Two boxes each containing 3 blocks of mass a, b and c
> are attached to the hinges of a door.   (8.11)

8.2 Possible Extensions

The following examples illustrate some phenomena that cannot currently be handled by the computer program. However, there seem to be no special reasons why they cannot be accommodated in our theoretical framework, and so it is conceivable that the program could be extended to handle them. (Of course, illusions of this kind can be quickly shattered as soon as a serious attempt is made at implementation.)

8.2.1 Complex Constraints on References

The mechanisms described for handling the interaction between 'each' phrases and other definite phrases are not adequate for some examples:

>   The man in each lift ...   (8.12)
>   The string attached to each pulley ...   (8.13)

In both of these, the initial noun phrase is normally read by a person as referring to a set of objects (or, rather, to the typical element of a set in the same way as an 'each' phrase does). However, our rules interpret it as referring to a single object that satisfies a set of constraints ('the man who is in each lift') rather than the preferred interpretation as a set of objects one for each of a set of constraints ('the men are in the lifts'). The correct interpretation seems to be very sensitive to the precise formulation of the relationship:

>   The string which is attached to each pulley ...   (8.14)

is often interpreted by people differently to (8.13) above, and in a way that corresponds to our rules. Somehow the system should be sensitive to these nuances. Vanlehn [Vanlehn 78] has made a more detailed analysis of examples such as this, but it seems to be impossible to form rigorous rules that have no significant counter-examples.

8.2.2 Sets of Sets

We have not by any means covered all the cases where noun phrases can invoke entities with multiple dependencies. One other place where this can happen involves the application of set-valued functions to sets of objects (see Appendix IV). An example is:

>   The ends of the three strings.   (8.15)

(where the function 'ends of' is applied to the set of strings). What should be invoked here (for the ends) seems to be an entity with two dependencies (each of the three strings has two ends). Or perhaps there should be just one dependency, with cardinality 6. A more thorough study needs to be made of how phrases such as this are used, in order that an appropriate representation can be chosen.

8.2.3 Questions and Commands

Our representation for the interpretations of indefinite noun phrases is totally geared towards being used for declarative sentences and cannot possibly suffice for questions or commands such as:

Is there a red pyramid on the table?   (8.16)

One simple possibility for extending the system would be to initially interpret questions and commands in the same way as statements, except for noting the different sentence type. The 'new' entities introduced could later be replaced by variables and the 'new' assertions used as a set of constraints to be used by a problem-solver or inference machine in answering the question or performing the command. For the example above, if the sentence 'There is a red pyramid on the table' gave rise to 'new' assertions:

    isa(pyramid,pyramid1)
    colour(pyramid1,red)
    on(pyramid1,table1)

then the question as stated would give rise to the goal:

Is there an X such that

    isa(pyramid,X)
    colour(X,red)
    on(X,table1)?

which would be more or less satisfactory. The application of this simple technique to sentences involving sets and quantification is, however, unlikely to be so straightforward. There is also the problem that the kinds of 'semantic checks' useful in the analysis of questions may bear little resemblance to those used for statements.

8.2.4 Subsequent Reference to 'Each' Phrases

One advantage of our explicit representation of dependencies in the composition of world model entities is that it makes available an extended range of things to be evoked by definite descriptions and pronouns (in the sense of [Webber 79]).

    10 men are standing in a lift.
    Each man weighs 100 lb.
    He also carries a 5 lb block.   (8.17)

Traditional approaches to quantification have had trouble accounting for the fact that the scope of 'each man' covers that of 'a 5 lb block', even though there is no quantifier in the third sentence. Our approach makes available a world model entity to be invoked by the pronoun ('#ref(2)', or whatever was used to represent 'each man') and the existing rules already specify that the block entity should inherit dependencies from it. It seems only to be necessary to make a change in the program so that the reference entity collecting candidates for 'he' can accept '#ref(2)' as one.†

8.3   Major Problems

The following examples demonstrate some of the basic lacks in the system. An attempt to deal with these would probably require a major revision to the basic framework.

8.3.1   Other Quantifiers

We have only dealt with restricted kinds of quantification—existential quantification and universal quantification over finite sets. The existing methods do not say much about how the following sentences could be analysed incrementally:

> Every string has two ends.
> Half of the people in the world are female.
> A string has two ends.
> An Atwood's machine is used to measure gravity.
> There are a few particles on the floor.   (8.18)

The first four sentences can all be seen as ways of using noun phrases to refer to (almost) infinite sets which are only known intensionally. Although the entities in our world model are intensional in some sense, they do not represent abstract, discourse-independent concepts, as we discussed in Section 4.5. We thus have no solution to the problem of representing the sets involved in these general laws. The final sentence introduces cardinality information of a very vague nature which is awkward to represent.

8.3.2   Complex Statements

In order to be able to build up meaning representations incrementally, we have had to make the basic assumption that the meaning of a sentence can be expressed as a conjunction of parts, each of which can be evaluated separately. In particular, we have not considered sentences with negation or other logical operators:

> The particle does not touch any point of the table.
> The ends of the string are not both fixed.   (8.19)

8.3.3   Selecting Subsets from Sets

There are many ways in English of expressing selections of elements from sets. Unfortunately it is not always clear how appropriate representations of vaguely specified subsets can be devised in a way that supports incremental interpretation.

---

† Since this section was written, this change has in fact been made successfully to the program.

One of the particles is fixed.
3 of the blocks weigh 5 lbs; another 5 weigh 10 lbs.   (8.20)

It is possible that making an arbitrary choice of which elements to select from the representation of the set may be a successful strategy. The general problem of maintaining cardinality information about a set given various descriptions of its subsets is difficult. Moreover, although our dependency list representation makes it possible to represent sets and individuals, it has no special facilities for representing arbitrary subsets.

Examples such as this point out a basic lack of flexibility in the dependency list representation, for a dependency list can only represent the structure of a set as a fixed collection of independent dimensions. If a set cannot be seen as the product of independent dependencies, it cannot be represented. Hence we cannot deal with a set which we only know about through the properties of arbitrary subsets. Perhaps extensions to the existing ideas will be able to handle this.

8.3.4 Non-referential Noun Phrases

This work has worked from the basic assumption that a noun phrase is referential, that is that it provides a description of a set of objects existing in the world. This assumption begins to break down when infinite sets are involved (Section 8.3.1), and is untenable for various non-specific uses of noun phrases.

John wants to marry a Swedish girl.
The string does not touch a wall.
John claimed to have seen a unicorn.   (8.21)

None of these sentences requires that there be a referent to the indefinite noun phrase in order for it to make sense. If 'referents' to such phrases are to be constructed in the way we have discussed, then at the very least it is necessary to qualify such entities with the scope of their existence (see [Woods 75]).

Chapter 9

CONCLUSIONS

Having surveyed the scope of our system through examples, let us now briefly review what this research set out to do and consider to what extent the aims have been achieved. The overall goal was to shed some light on the (somewhat vague) question 'How much early semantic analysis is it feasible to build into a computer program?'. In order to study this, we looked at existing attempts to carry out 'early' interpretation of noun phrases. These had to face the problem of local uncertainty in semantic analysis—the problem that the significance of a fragment of text may not be apparent until it is seen in the context of a larger fragment. In such situations, the only hope for early semantic analysis seemed to be to make arbitrary decisions and be prepared to backtrack. In response to this problem, we developed a system of *incremental* reference evaluation. This allowed early semantic interpretation to cope successfully with:

— cases where the referents of definite phrases can only be obtained by consideration of global constraints generated after the phrases are read;
— cases where the cardinality of sets introduced by indefinite noun phrases can only be obtained by consideration of semantic relationships with other noun phrases occurring later.

By using representations for the kinds of partial information available in these cases we were able to construct a system that could continue reliably with semantic analysis through the uncertainties. Having done this, we should now look briefly at the question 'What has this shown about the feasibility of early semantic analysis in general?'

An important thing that has become clear is that there is no simple answer about what is possible and what is not. The problems for early semantic analysis that we considered were only problems for its efficiency—none of the examples we looked at presented any absolute obstacle to it. Of course, they introduced uncertainties that would have severely restricted the usefulness of any computer program pursuing a naive approach. However, the only reason that we saw the examples as restricting the feasibility of early semantic analysis was because a straightforward attack would have been extremely inefficient and would have offered an inappropriate way of tackling them. All that we have managed to show is that a more considered approach to early semantic analysis, making use of partial information and avoiding arbitrary decisions, can overcome these particular search problems. It maybe introduces other search problems (in the inference system), but it does seem to offer a reasonable and feasible alternative. Unfortunately, the feasibility of early semantic analysis can only be estimated by informal and intuitive arguments about the relative efficiency of different programs.

Another reason why a simple answer is not possible is that it all depends on what depth of semantic analysis is to be involved. Naive approaches to early semantic analysis fail on the problems we have considered because they insist on an over-detailed level of interpretation before the requisite information is available. We have shown that much of semantic analysis can take place at more abstract levels, independent of decisions that are to be made about the low-level details. So the choice of an appropriate depth of analysis is very important for determining how much early semantic analysis is feasible. We have attempted to find an approach that does not lose any flexibility when it chooses an abstract level to work at—this has been motivated by the desire to have available semantic checks of some complexity. Unfortunately, this means that sometimes early decisions have to be made when analysis at an abstract level needs more details than it can provide. Examples of this are the places where 'questions' force choices about referents and plural definite references have to be 'finalised'. If we had been content with a more superficial semantic analysis (in terms of semantic markers, say) then it might not have been necessary for even these choices to be made.

Our approach has been to assume that a deep level of semantic analysis is given, and then to try to find out what degree of early semantic analysis is feasible. We have been able to push out the boundaries further than originally appeared possible. Questions of reference evaluation and logical quantification seemed to present serious search problems for early semantic analysis. However, we have shown that the use of appropriate representations allows some of these problems to be neatly solved. We have had to make strong assumptions, for instance about referentiality and finiteness, but perhaps later work will be able to push back the frontiers even further. It is especially important that the efficient implementation of inferences involving partially-specified or intensionally-defined entities be investigated—we have only begun to consider some of the problems in Chapter 7.

Some of the ideas which this research has thrown up are interesting in their own right and may be useful even outside the context of early semantic analysis:

— The idea of seeing reference evaluation as a constraint satisfaction task. This would seem to be appropriate whenever complex criteria of semantic well-formedness are allowed to have an influence on it. Thus some of our methods could also be applied in a system that postponed reference evaluation until a late stage.
— The idea of representing quantifier scope as dependencies between complex entities in the world model. This might provide the basis for a new approach to quantification that could handle troublesome issues such as pronominal reference to 'each' phrases. This remains to be properly investigated.
— The idea of representing sets that cannot conveniently be enumerated by using typical elements, with an extra level of information about what kind of sets they correspond to. This is obviously more generally applicable (although the basic concept is not original with us), and might even be extended to deal with infinite sets.

Finally, it is hoped that some of the points that we have made about the treatment of definite reference and phrases describing sets may have clarified some of the important issues and made some useful distinctions. This might include the notion of 'broken' and 'unbroken' entities and the two kinds of definite reference to sets.

Chapter 10

POSTSCRIPT

This book is based on work which I carried out at the University of Edinburgh between about 1978 and 1981. A considerable amount of progress has been made within the field of natural language processing and neighbouring fields since 1981, and I have attempted to include in a limited way references to later work within the main part of the text. This postscript provides a selective account of recent work in natural language processing that has a bearing on the problems addressed in the book.

10.1 Syntactic Parsing

Although syntactic processing was not a particular theoretical interest for our computer program, having decided to implement a parser in the most straightforward way allowed by Prolog, we ended up with something similar in spirit to many ATN systems. That is, the parser used a depth-first search through alternatives, using chronological backtracking and a largely top-down approach. Although the ATN approach was at one time that favoured by most computational linguists, in recent days other parsing ideas have come to the fore.

One rival approach, that of 'deterministic parsing', as pioneering by Marcus, has been mentioned briefly in the text. To simplify greatly, deterministic parsing seeks to solve search problems by postponing decisions and making use of limited lookahead within the sentence. It can be argued that imposing particular restrictions on lookahead gives rise to a parsing system that has many of the characteristics of the 'human parser'. Marcus's work is very similar to ours in its approach to search. That is, a deterministic parser's ability to postpone decisions until relevant information has been obtained can be compared directly with the notion of producing a partial representation of some ambiguous referent and gradually refining it as time goes on. A later version of our program did in fact run in conjunction with a deterministic parser, written by Rob Milne [Milne 83], although the interface was not a 'tightly coupled' one.

The other main parsing approach now favoured by computational linguists is that of 'chart parsing', developed by Kay [Kay 80] (although many of the ideas were present in earlier work of Kay and Kaplan). Simplifying again, the chart enables a parser to keep track of constituents found ('well formed substrings') and parsing goals in such a way as to avoid useless duplication of effort. In particular, it enables independent choices to be treated independently. Again, there are similarities with our approach to noun phrases. It is only possible to survive with a partially determined referent if the subsequent processing is largely independent of the choices still to be made about that referent. Our representation of referents by candidate sets and our use of filtering techniques can be seen as simply a device to enable independent choices to be made independently. It would be interesting therefore to see whether our ideas can be extended to the maintenance of a general 'semantic chart' holding 'well formed semantic structures' of some kind. Such an enterprise might be able to make use of Warren's notion of Earley deduction and techniques for recording the dependence of choices as used in Doyle's TMS [Doyle 79].

In summary, there is now a rich set of mechanisms for handling search in syntactic parsing. A very useful contribution could be made by somebody determining the extent to which these could be employed to solve search problems in semantic and discourse-level analysis.

10.2 Syntactic/Semantic Scheduling

We have presented a model of syntax/semantics interaction in language understanding, using the notion that 'semantic operations' are invoked at appropriate points in the syntactic analysis. In many ways, our model lacked precision in its specification of what the appropriate points were and what the information passed between syntactic and semantic processes was. This was largely a reflection of the focus of the work, but was also partly due to the fact that an elegant formalism for describing this did not seem to exist. Woods's 'cascaded ATNs' [Woods 80] provide a clear way of specifying multiple ATN systems, where the 'output' of one ATN forms the 'input' of another. In an implementation of cascaded ATNs, the separate ATNs may run in parallel, each one being able to continue just as long as it has available input. It may be that cascaded ATNs would provide a good notation for describing our system, with the syntactic and semantic components each described as a separate 'ATN'. Nevertheless, there are certainly some changes that would need to be made to Woods's formalism as it stands [Christaller and Metzing 83]. An alternative strategy would be to conceive of the whole system as a logic program with certain conjunctions of goals executed in parallel. That is, I could provide a logical description of the relationship between a sentence and its possible parse trees and also the relationship between the parse trees and their possible interpretations. This would then be executed with suitable control annotations to ensure that the syntactic and semantic processing would be interleaved. There are now logic programming languages, such as PARLOG [Clark and Gregory 81] and Concurrent Prolog [Shapiro 83], where such control strategies can be imposed. We have already suggested [Mellish 83a] that the difference between conventional and 'semantically based' parsers can be seen purely in terms of control strategy, rather than in terms of the underlying logic.

10.3 Semantic Representations

One possible source of support for a model of natural language understanding based on incremental semantic interpretation would be psychological evidence. A major contribution to Cognitive Science was made by Johnson-Laird's book *Mental Models* [Johnson-Laird 83] which appeared after our work, and it is worthwhile to consider what (if any), compatibilities there are between our own and Johnson-Laird's theories. The major thrust of Johnson-Laird's approach in fact contradicts the idea of incremental semantic interpretation as we have construed it. For he sees the process of comprehension as involving the construction of a single mental model, even if the discourse does not provide enough information to determine it uniquely. If the discourse is imprecise or ambiguous, the comprehension system thus builds a single precise model, even if it must make arbitrary assumptions in the process. On the other hand, if this model turns out to be inadequate, it can be recursively revised in the light of subsequent discourse. So semantic interpretation for people is not incremental—there is no means within mental models of representing partially-determined situations, and the system must at all times have a completely-specified model of the situation. Presumably the 'recursive revision' processes look somewhat like Doyle's truth maintenance. Although Johnson-Laird's basic thesis contradicts our notion of incremental interpretation, he does outline other possible ways in which people seem to represent indeterminate discourse, apart from choosing a single mental model. One of these involves 'representing indeterminacy within a mental model by introducing a propositional-like element of notation'. Johnson-Laird's examples of this are very much in the same spirit as the partial representations used in this book.

Many meaning representations used by AI researchers are inspired by the precision and well-foundedness of logic-like notations. Moreover, much of the emphasis in AI work on knowledge representation is on finding ways to represent more kinds of things, rather than on looking for representations that support incremental refinement. It follows that recent developments in semantic representation do not seem to bear much on our problems. One development that does, however, offer promise is Barwise and Perry's [Barwise and Perry 83] 'situation semantics'. Barwise and Perry seem to take seriously the problem of dealing with partially determined 'situations', and it will be a valuable exercise to determine how their theories relate to the problems of ambiguity in semantic interpretation.

10.4 Pragmatics of Language Use

In Chapter 4, we touched briefly on the issue of the beliefs of the speaker and hearer in a natural language conversation. We pointed out that certain syntactic markings indicate beliefs that the speaker has about the beliefs of the hearer. Since these will not necessarily coincide with the actual beliefs of the hearer, the hearer must be somewhat tolerant, in particular as regards which objects (s)he regards as distinct at different times. Our account of the role of beliefs in natural language communication was necessarily sketchy, and recent work has provided important new insights into this fascinating area. Some researchers, for instance Clark and Marshall [Clark and Marshall 78] have investigated the theoretical requirements for successful communication. Others have investigated how speech acts can be planned to achieve goals specified in terms of beliefs [Cohen 78] and indeed how particular referential acts can be chosen in a goal-oriented manner [Appelt 81]. From the other direction, Allen's work [Allen 83] investigates how intentions and beliefs of the speaker may be inferred from his/her utterances. Shadbolt [Shadbolt 85] produces a model in which one can express interpretations of sentences where different terms are interpreted relative to different belief contexts. It would be interesting to see to what extent our naive treatment of beliefs could be 'cleaned up' into a system that reasoned rigorously about such issues.

10.5 Incremental Semantic Interpretation

Since the work described in this book was completed, we have done some limited further work on incremental semantic representations. One limitation that we have felt is the need (in the approach described here) to keep explicit candidate sets for ambiguous referents, especially as these sets might be rather large in some situations. We have thus investigated a scheme [Mellish 82] where as an alternative the constraints on the referents are stored directly. These constraints will only be activated to choose the referent when they are guaranteed to have at most one solution. Although this scheme has some attractions, it is a significant problem to determine whether an arbitrary conjunction of constraints is guaranteed to have at most one solution. The system as implemented is conservative in that, if in doubt, it will simply keep a set of constraints stored up without investigating possible solutions. This means that inconsistent sets of constraints may not be detected until a long time after they are created, and this is obviously undesirable. For a subset of possible constraints, type constraints, we have therefore implemented a special-purpose inference system that can incrementally refine a description of the type of a constrained object in such a way that an inconsistent type constraint is immediately detected. This approach is closely related to Frisch's use of sorted logic to reduce search in parsing [Frisch 85]. It would be interesting to investigate whether other special-purpose inference systems [Bundy et al., 82] could be devised for other special classes of constraints.

Radically different ideas about the process of semantic interpretation are inspired by the concept of connectionist machines [Hinton and Anderson 81]. Cottrell and Small [Cottrell and Small 83] and Waltz and Pollack [Waltz and Pollack 84] both present schemes which allow word senses to be smoothly disambiguated as a sentence is read. In a sense, these are implementations of the 'semantic chart' idea mentioned above, except that alternative possible interpretations are allowed to locally activate and inhibit one another in the search for a globally 'best' solution. Since these two systems only deal with word senses, they can also be seen as a reimplementation of Wilks's 'preference semantics', which was likewise tolerent of mild semantic anomaly and aimed for a globally 'preferred' solution. What is not at all clear is whether these connectionist models can be straightforwardly extended to deal with semantic interpretation at the discourse level (e.g. reference). If they can be, then it is not unlikely that they will end up with representations similar to those developed in our work.

Appendices

Appendix I

CONSTRAINT SATISFACTION ALGORITHM (See Section 3.4)

I.1   Reference Entities

Associated with a reference entity are various features that summarise the state of evaluation and facilitate constraint satisfaction. We will use the following notation for these:

A reference entity r has at any point in time the attributes:

— cands(r)—a set of admissible candidates
— num(r)—a number expressing the minimum number of candidates that are expected to be valid
— constr(r)—a set of constraints on possible values of r
— var(r)—a 'dedicated variable' that stands for r in the propositions of constr(r)
— ment(r)—the set of other reference entities mentioned in constr(r)

These features have all been introduced in Chapter 3 except for 'var'. It is essential to know what part r plays in the constraints of 'constr(r)', and this can be marked in the propositions either by the name of r (e.g. 'ref(23)') or by any other token specific to r. Since we will require the ability to 'instantiate' this with possible candidates, it seems best to conceptualise this token as a variable.

I.2   Global Variables

The algorithm will make use of two global variables:

— 'Todo'—the set of reference entities whose candidates are to be reconsidered.
— 'Changed'—a flag indicating whether a change has occurred in the most recently considered candidate set.

I.3   Algorithm to Satisfy a Constraint C

Note that this and the next sections owe much to existing work on constraint satisfaction.

Preliminaries:

> Let R be the set of reference entities occurring in C.
> Let C' be C with every occurring reference r replaced by its
>> own variable var(r).
> If $|R| = 0$, fail if C' cannot be proved; otherwise succeed.

Storing constraints:

> If $|R| > 1$,
>> For each r in R,
>>> constr(r) ← constr(r) U $\{C'\}$,
>>> ment(r) ← ment(r) U (R–r)

Main filtering:

> Todo ← O,
> For each r in R,
>> Filter r with respect to $\{C'\}$
>> (this may change Todo)

> Until Todo = O,
>> Select r in Todo,
>> Todo ← Todo-r,
>> Filter r with respect to constr(r)

I.4   To Filter an Entity r with Respect to Constraints Cs

Changed ← false,
For each c in cand(r),

> Instantiate var(r) with c,
> If the conjunction of Cs can be deduced such that

For each r′ in ment(r) there is c′ in cands(r′)
  such that
var(r′) is instantiated consistently as c′

then OK
Otherwise,

  cand(r) ← cand(r)–c,
  Changed ← true

Clear all variable instantiations

If | cand(r) | < num(r), fail.
If Changed, Todo ← Todo U ment(r).

Appendix II

SUMMARY OF RULES ABOUT DEPENDENCY LISTS

In the main part of this book, rules have been given for the formation of dependency lists for entities in the world model and for manipulations on these to obtain the effects of interacting sets and quantifiers. These can now be brought together and summarised.

II.1 Initial Values of Dependency Lists

The initial values of the dependency lists of entities depend on the kinds of phrases that they arise from, as follows:

— Singular indefinite noun phrase. The entity arising initially has an empty dependency list.
— Plural indefinite noun phrase. The entity has a single dependency, named 'external'. This is 'unused' and has whatever number information is given in the phrase (see Section 4.3).
— Singular definite noun phrase. The reference entity has the same dependencies as whichever candidate is the 'correct' one.
— Plural definite noun phrase. In its initial 'given' environment the entity behaves as the last case above. When it emerges into a 'new' environment, it becomes either a reference entity (as the last case) or a special set entity. In the second case, it has one dependency ('external'), which is 'used' and has the same number as the number of remaining candidates (see Section 5.1).
— Simple or compound modifier. A simple modifier has no dependencies. A compound modifier behaves as a set entity.

— 'Each' phrase. The referent is the same as that of the corresponding set phrase. However, it is marked so that the 'external' dependency is seen by the semantic preprocessors as being named after the entity itself (see Section 5.2).

II.2 Binary Matching Operations on Dependency Lists

The following rules capture all the individual mechanisms described earlier for binary operations. They thus include 'external pairing' and the effects of universal quantification (to the extent that has been discussed here).

The execution of a binary semantic operation consists of the following manipulation on the dependency lists of the participating entities followed by the invocation of the appropriate semantic routine for 'corresponding' pairs of entities.

— Any dependencies which appear under the same name in both lists should immediately share all information (number and usage) and in addition be linked together.
— If an indefinite entity is involved, it must inherit all those non-'external' dependencies that it does not already have from the other entity.

II.3 Generating 'Corresponding Pairs'

Given entities p, q, the combination $\langle p', q' \rangle$ is generated if:

There is a function f: Dependencies → Integers U Variables such that:

If d1 and d2 are linked dependencies, f(d1) = f(d2).
If d is a broken dependency, $1 \leq f(d) \leq$ number of d.
If d is an unbroken dependency, f(d) is in Variables

and

p' is the realisation of p under f.
q' is the realisation of q under f.

An entity X is the realisation of entity Y
under function F if:

Y is set (N) with dependency d, F(d) = n
and the nth member of set(N) is X

or

Y is ref(N), Y plural, Z is the valid candidate of Y
and X is Z under F

or

Y is ref(N), Y singular and X is ref(N)

or

Y is #Z and X is Z under F

or
    Y is an indefinite entity,
        Z is the incarnation of Y
        with respect to its dependency list and F,
        and X is Z with trailing variables removed.

    Z is the incarnation of Y with respect to L and F if:

        L is 'nil' and Z is Y
or
        The first element of L is d and
            Z is the incarnation of Y.F(d) with respect to
            the rest of L and F

MEANINGS OF PREDICATES USED IN EXAMPLES

The following are the main predicates used in examples in this book. Explanations have been provided so as to make the examples more understandable, and not because there is any great significance in the precise predicates or where they are used. Indeed, most of the examples only incorporate a 'toy' semantic analysis meant to suggest a more complete treatment but not to overwhelm the reader with details.

III.1 Main Predicates

isa(A,B)—
> Object B is idealised as having type A.

hasname (A,B)—
> Object B has been mentioned with noun A.

length(A,B,C)—
> The length of object A is quantity B at time C.

mass(A,B,C)—
> The mass of object A is quantity B at time C.

coeff(A,B,C)—
> The coefficient of friction of object A is quantity B
> at time C.

fixed(A)—
> Object A occupies a fixed location.

uniform(A)—
> Object A is uniform.

measure(A,B,C)—
>Quantity A has number B in units C.

supports(A,B)—
>Object A supports object B.

contact(A,B,C)—
>Object A is in contact with object B at time C.

fixed_contact(A,B,C)—
>Object A is fixed to and in contact with object B
>at time C.

point_of(A,B)—
>Object B is a point of object A.

end(A,B,C)—
>Object B is the end of object A of type C
>(C is left or right).

midpt(A,B)—
>Object B is the midpoint of object A.

hinge(A,B,C)—
>Object B is the hinge of object A of type C
>(C is up or down).

III.2   Predicates Used for 'Semantic Tests'

tsatisfies(A,B)—
>Object B has property A.

tctrgravity(A,B)—
>Object A's centre of gravity is given by the part B.

thaspart(A,B)—
>Object A can have a part of type B.

mentioned(A,B)—
>Object A has been mentioned with plurality B.

tshape(A,B)—
>Object A has shape B.

separable(A,B)—
>Objects A and B are not fixed relative to one another.

contactpt(A,B)—
>One possible point for making contact with object A
>is given by part B.

diff(A,B)—
>A and B are different objects.

vacant(A)—
>Object A is not in fixed contact with anything.

A NOTE ON FUNCTIONS

There are various reasons why it is necessary to take special account of nouns which name 'functions'. However, since a discussion of this issue does not belong in the main development of the book, it has been postponed until this appendix.

The first point to make is that functions provide an important exception to our simplified rule for determining given/new status. Thus in:

What is the mass of the particle?

the noun phrase 'the mass . . .' is definite, but may not be referring to an individual explicitly encountered before. The definite article can be used here because there is always a guarantee that the value of a function (here, the function of mass) exists and is unique for each possible argument (here, the particle). In the computer program, there is a special mechanism for functions which looks to see if a function value is already known. If so, the referent of the noun phrase is known to be an entity coextensive with the existing one. Otherwise an entity assumed to correspond to a new object is created.

When a function can have sets as its values, an element of a particular value is often referred to with the indefinite article:

An end of the string.

Since every string is guaranteed to have a unique set of two ends, 'the ends of' can be seen as a function which, given a string as its argument, produces a set of two ends as its result. In this phrase, one of the elements of such a set is being selected. The phrase would sound quite reasonable even if we were already acquainted with both of the ends. However, this contradicts our rule that expects indefinite articles to introduce 'new' objects. Once again, a special mechanism is necessary. The use of the indefinite article to select an element from a known set seems to be confined to function values—for other sets, formulations such as 'one_' and 'one of the _s' seem more natural. We discuss the problems associated with selecting elements from known sets briefly in Section 8.3.3.

The second point of interest about functions is that the entity representing the value of a function usually needs to inherit a certain amount of the extra information known about the function argument. Thus 'the mass of 2 particles' refers to a set in the same way as '2 particles' does. Also, a function applied to a reference entity must have as its candidates the values of the function when applied to that entity's candidates. In the program, when an entity representing the value of a function is created, the entity is made according to the 'pattern' specified by the argument entity. If the argument is a reference entity, then it will be also, each dependency of the argument will give rise to a dependency of the function value, and so on.

It is interesting that the set of functions available is not independent of the context of the text. Thus, although some functions (such as 'mass' and 'velocity') are known about in advance, some may only come to exist through the recognition of standard situations. For instance, the use of the definite article for the particles in:

In an Atwood's machine the particles have . . .   (9.1)

(from [Street 29]) is possible because the context has already established the existence and uniqueness of two particles. These can perhaps be regarded as 'functions of the situation'. We have not yet investigated this fully.

Appendix V

PROGRAM DESCRIPTION

This appendix describes the implementation of the program referred to in the body of the book, and includes some excerpts from the code. The reader is assumed to be familiar with Prolog, the syntax of Dec10 Prolog and the syntax of Prolog grammar rules (DCGs). Some of the examples have been cleaned up and simplified slightly for the sake of clarity (the total program occupies over 40 pages of code). A description of an earlier version of the program is to be found in [Mellish 78], which also goes into more detail about some parts of the syntactic analysis.

V.1 Introduction

The program described here was designed to read in mechanics problems stated in English and convert them into a formal representation that could be used by a problem-solving program [Bundy *et al.*, 79]. This program was not written entirely by the author—the verb routines and semantic operations were written by Martha Palmer. However, this appendix will concentrate on those aspects which have most to do with the rest of the book.

V.2 Basic Strategy

In the program, partial results of semantic analysis, as well as other global information about the input, are stored in a special datastructure associated with the current clause. Structures of this kind are passed as arguments to most procedures in the program, and are generally denoted by the variable 'X'. The internal form of a clause datastructure is described in

Section V.9. The basic idea is that at any stage there will be many uninstantiated variables in this structure. As the program discovers more about the input, some of these variables become instantiated, possibly with complex values that themselves contain uninstantiated variables. So the clause datastructure will gradually express more and more information through the process of becoming progressively more defined. At the end, there may still be uninstantiated variables, but it is known that no more information will arise. At this point, the important parts of the structure are printed out to form the program's output.

Another argument that is passed to many procedures is the flag recording whether the current phrase is conveying 'given' or 'new' information—this has the value 'test' or 'add' correspondingly. This flag is normally denoted by the variable 'F'.

V.3 Top Level Control

The main flow of control of the program is determined by the state of the syntactic analysis of the input. Syntactic analysis is interleaved with semantic analysis, inasmuch as semantic interpretation of a fragment generally follows directly on the determination of the syntactic structure. Therefore it is not surprising that the top level of the program is formulated as grammar rules. Fig. V.1 shows the code for dealing with a single clause of the input (predicate 'sentence'). The procedure is to simply find constituents ('O') in the clause, interpreting them appropriately, until something like a full stop appears. At this point, the main verb is retrieved and a semantic routine associated with it is called.

```
sentence(F,X) --> readcons(F,X).

   readcons(F,X) --> constituent(O,F,X), action(O,F,X).

   action(binder:B,F,X)   -->  !, binder(B,F,X).
   action(O,F,X)          -->  readcons(F,X).

   binder('.',F,X)          -->  {level(X,0)}, !, {endofsent(F,X)}.
   binder('.',F,X), ['.']   -->  {endofsent(F,X)}.

endofsent(F,X) :- clearuproles(X), testrole(mainverb,V,X),
              Goal=.. [V,F,X], call(Goal).
```

Fig. V.1 – Top level control

V.4 Syntactic Roles

The interpretations of the main constituents of a clause are assigned syntactic roles which will be used by the verb routines. The main procedures that manipulate syntactic roles are:

— newrole(R,C,X)—store value C under role R in X,
— testrole(R,C,X)—return the value C recorded under role Ṛ (failing if there is not one),
— closerole(R,X)—make the value recorded under role R invisible to future 'testrole' operations,
— clearuproles(X)—clear up the roles at the end of a clause.

V.5   Constituent Analysis

The result of interpreting a constituent is a structure of the form Y:G, where Y is a type indication and G is a semantically meaningful value. The types are simple syntactic identifiers (such as 'binder', 'verbgr'), except that a more detailed breakdown of noun phrases than usual is carried out. Thus a noun phrase referring to a physical object gives rise to type 'physobj' whereas a phrase such as 'the mass of the particle' gives rise to type

```
constituent(Y:G,F,X) -->
    first(A,C,X),
    {accommodate(A,Y:G,X)},
    second(C,Y,G1,F,X),
    and(Y,G1,G,F,X).

    first(np,indefsp,X)              --> [a].
    first(np,defsp,X)                --> [the].
    first(np,physobj:G,X)            --> [it],
                                         {test(mentioned(G,sing),X)}.
    first(pp(P),findpobj,X)          --> [P], {prep(P,_,_)}.
    first(aux,aux:A,X)               --> [A], {aux(A)}.
    first(binder,binder:B,X)         --> [B], {binder(B)}.
    first(verbgr,verbgr:I,X)         --> verbgr(I,X).

    accommodate(np,O,X)                     :- presubst(O,X).
    accommodate(pp(P),pobject:O,X)  :- dprep(P,X), newrole(pp(P),O,X).

      presubst(O,X) :- testrole(mainverb,I,X), !, saftermv(O,X).
      presubst(O,X) :- testrole(hv,Hv,X), !, safterhv(O,X).
      presubst(O,X) :- newrole(subject,O,X).

      dprep(P,X) :- (testrole(mainverb,V,X) -> prefor(V,P); true).

    second(Y:G,Y,G,W,W) :- !.
    second(C,Y,G,F,X,W1,W2) ;-
        C=..[N | As],
        append(As,[Y,G,F,X,W1,W2],A1),
        L=..[N | A1],      call(L).
```

Fig. V.2 – Constituent analysis

'defmeas' ('definite measure'). These types are specific to the mechanics domain and enable a certain amount of case analysis on constituents to be done by pattern matching. The analysis of a constituent takes place in two stages (Fig. V.2). This technique apparently has some similarities with 'left corner parsing'. First of all, the next word or words in the input string are examined to determine what kind of constituent comes next (the first argument returned by 'first'). Then an appropriate 'top down' routine (the second argument returned by 'first') is called to finish off the work. Between, what will be the new constituent's interpretation is accommodated into the set of filled syntactic roles (with failure occurring if this cannot be done). (If the interpretation can be finished in the first stage, the second argument of 'first' returns this and the second stage is avoided.) Finally, a general routine 'and' investigates whether the constituent found was in fact the first of a conjunction of phrases of this type.

Fig. V.3 and V.4 show two of the routines for anaysing constituents.
'verbgr' parses a main verb group (incorporating a previously found auxiliary—hv—if necessary), to get the root V(erb), T(ense) (past, present or future), A(spect) (continuing, instant or completed), M(ood) (active or passive) and N(umber) (singular or plural). In fact, of these, only V, M and N are used.

'defsp' analyses a noun phrase that has begun with 'the' (a proper definite noun phrase). The first three clauses deal with phrases such as 'the former', 'the other end of the string' and 'the mass of the particle', respectively. The fourth deals with the more normal definite noun phrase. An optional number is read, then the pre-nominal adjectives are collected up until a common noun ('class' name) is found. After the referent has been created (in 'np', which 'gensym's a token if the environment is 'add' but otherwise merely provides a constraint on the value), the semantics of these adjectives are invoked and then all 'post adjectives' are dealt with. The second 'postadj' clause shows the treatment of one kind of relative clause. A new 'clause datastructure' Y is derived from X, and eventually the 'sentence' predicate will be invoked recursively with one of the syntactic roles already filled.

Before we look in more detail at how the semantic routines are invoked, we should have a brief look at how the dictionary is organised: see Fig. V.5.
The task of the dictionary is always to answer questions of the form 'is word X of category Y?' and not 'what is the category of word X?'. It thus suffices to have it indexed on the syntactic categories. Regular words in root form, as well as irregular forms, are dealt with by simple lookup. Regular inflections (for possessives, past particles, etc.) are treated by more complex routines, which try to decompose a word into a known root with a given ending.

The dictionary incorporates a crude analysis of which prepositions are expected to appear with which verbs (predicate 'prepfor').

```
verbgr(mainverb(V,[N,M,T,A]),X) -->
   {testrole(hv,A1,X), !, closerole(hv,X)},
   push(A1), vg(V,T,A,M,N).
verbgr(mainverb(V,[N,M,T,A]),X) -->
   vg(V,T,A,M,N).

vg(V,fut,A,M,N)              -->   [will], inf(V,A,M).
vg(V,pres,A,M,sing)         -->   [is], papr(V,A,M).
vg(V,pres,A,M,plur)         -->   [are], papr(V,A,M).
vg(V,past,A,M,sing)         -->   [was], papr(V,A,M).
vg(V,past,A,M,plur)         -->   [were], papr(V,A,M).
vg(V,pres,compl,M,sing)     -->   [has], pa(V,M).
vg(V,pres,compl,M,plur)     -->   [have], pa(V,M).
vg(V,past,compl,M,N)        -->   [had], pa(V,M).
vg(V,pres,inst,actv,sing)   -->   [does,V], {verb(V)}.
vg(V,pres,inst,actv,plur)   -->   [do,V], {verb(V)}.
vg(V,past,inst,actv,N)      -->   [did,V], {verb(V)}.
vg(V,pres,inst,actv,N)      -->   [P], {pres(P,V,N)}.
vg(V,past,inst,actv,N)      -->   [P], {past(P,V)}.

papr(V,cing,passv)     -->   [being,P], {pastpart(P,V)}.
papr(V,inst,passv)     -->   [P], {pastpart(P,V)}.
papr(V,cing,actv)      -->   [P], {prespart(P,V)}.

pa(V,passv)     -->   [been,P], {pastpart(P,V)}.
pa(V,actv)      -->   [P], {pastpart(P,V)}.

inf(V,compl,M)      -->   [have], pa(V,M).
inf(V,A,M)          -->   [be], papr(V,A,M).
inf(V,inst,actv)    -->   [V], {verb(V)}.
```

Fig. V.3 – Verb group parsing

V.6 Semantic Verb Routines

When the main constituents of a clause have been interpreted, a routine named after the main verb is called to investigate the semantics of the clause as a whole. Examples of such routines are given in Fig. V.6. The function of a verb routine is to access the filled syntactic roles, determine the appropriate sense of the verb and then invoke more primitive semantic operations to express the meaning. There may be several Prolog clauses for a single verb, as in the example for 'be' here. The appropriate clause will be chosen by a mixture of pattern-matching of types and by the success or failure of 'semantic checks' on the semantic operations.

```
defsp(physobj,G,F,X) --> [former], !, {forlat(1,X,G)}.
defsp(Y,G,F,X)        --> [other], !, part(P,one), ofobj(G1,F,X),
                              {postpart(P,other,G1,G,test,X)}.
defsp(defmeas,G,F,X) --> dim(D,_), !, ofobj(G1,F,X),
                              {disfn(G1,D,F,X,G)}.
defsp(Y,G1,F,X)       --> (([N], {num(N,L)}); []),
                              physobj(L,S,H,G,test,X),
                              postphysobj(H,G,Y,G1,F,X).

   physobj(L,S,H,G,F,X) --> getadjs(As),
                              [C], {class(C,C1,[S,H])}.
                              {np(G,L,C1,F,X)},
                              {doadjs(As,G,F,X)},
                              postadjs(F,physobj:G,X).

np(G,L,C,add,X) :- gensym(C,G), newindef(G,L,X),
                        distrib([C],G,makenoun,add,X).
np(G,L,C,test,X) :- test(hasname(C,R),X).

doadjs([],_,_,_).
doadjs([A | As],G,F,X) :- distrib([A],G,makeadj,F,X),
                              doadjs(As,G,F,X).

postadj(F,Y:G1,X)     --> [P], {prep(P,s,_)},
                              parse(physobj:G,F,X),
                              {distrib(G1,G,P,F,X)}.
postadj(F,O,X)        --> [P,R], {prep(P,_,_), relpron(R)},
                              {matchsent(X,Y), newrole(pp,pp(P,O),Y)},
                              subsentence(F,X,Y).

postphysobj(poss,G1,defmeas,G2,F,X) -->
   dim(D,_), {disfn(G1,D,F,X,G2)}.
postphysobj(noposs,G1,physobj,G1,F,X).
```

Fig. V.4 – Proper definite noun phrases

V.7   Semantic Preprocessing

All access to the basic semantic operations is through the 'semantic preprocessors'. In the program, both single objects and typical elements of sets
are represented by single Prolog terms. Those corresponding to sets are
distinguished because they have non-trivial 'dependency lists' saying what
kinds of sets they are (see Section V.10). Effects of quantifier scope can be
obtained by adding appropriately to this information. The semantic preprocessors handle the necessary copying and matching of dependency
information and also expand out operations on sets into operations on
'unbroken' entities (roughly, into operations on the representations of
single objects). The two main types of call to the semantic preprocessors

```
class(pier).
class(ball).
class(rod).

class(men,man,[plur,noposs]).
class(boxes,box,[plur,noposs]).

class(C,C,[sing,noposs]) :- class(C).
class(C1,C2,[S,P]) :-
    name(C1,X1), ending(X1,X2,S,P),
    name(C2,X2), class(C2).

    ending("'s",[],sing,poss).
    ending("s",[],plur,noposs).
    ending("s'",[],plur,poss).
    ending("'",[],sing,poss).
    ending([L | Ls],[L | Ms],S,P) :- ending(Ls,Ms,S,P).

verb(contain).
verb(attach).

pastpart(hung,hang).

pastpart(P,V) :- name(P,X),
    (append(Z,"ed",X); append(Z,"en",X)),
    verbdb(Z,V).

prep(into,d,loc).
prep(over,s,loc).
prep(with,s,noloc).

prepfor(suspend,from).
prepfor(rest,on).
prepfor(be,loc).

prepfor(V,P) :- prep(P,_,loc), prepfor(V,loc).
```

Fig. V.5 – Dictionary extract

are as follows:

1. distrib(Entity1,Entity2,Key,F,X).
2. disfn(Entity,Key,F,X,Result).

In each of these, the argument 'Key' is the name of the semantic operation to be invoked. Examples are 'makeadj' (apply the meaning of an adjective), 'makenoun' (apply the meaning of a noun), any preposition or the name of a specific relation ('makecontact' names the routine dealing with the proposition that two objects are in contact). 'distrib' deals with a rela-

```
connect(F,X) :-
    logsubj(physobj:Str,X),
    logobj(physobj:Objs,X),
    disfn(Str,end,F,X,Ends),
    distrib(Objs,Ends,makecontact,F,X).

be(F,X) :-
    logsubj(defmeas:M,X),
    logobj(measpair:P,X), !,
    distrib(M,P,breakdown,F,X).
be(F,X) :-
    logsubj(physobj:S,X),
    logobj(adj:A,X), !,
    distrib([A],S,makeadj,F,X).
be(F,X) :-
    logsubj(physobj:S,X),
    applypps(S,F,X).

    logsubj(O,X) :- ismood(actv,X), testrole(subject,O,X).
    logsubj(O,X) :- ismood(passv,X), pp(by,O,X).

    logobj(O,X) :- ismood(actv,X), testrole(object#1,O,X).
    logobj(O,X) :- ismood(passv,X), testrole(subject,O,X).

    pp(P,O,X) :- testrole(pp(P),O,X), closerole(pp(P),X).

    applypps(S,F,X) :- pp(P,physobj:O,X), !,
        distrib(S,O,P,F,X), applypps(S,F,X).
    applypps(_,_,_).
```

Fig. V.6 – Example verb routines

tion between two entities (one of which may be simply a modifier or list of modifiers), and 'disfn' deals with obtaining the value when a function is applied to an entity. We will look at 'distrib' in slightly more detail. The first stage of semantic preprocessing involves looking at the dependency lists of the two entities. If both entities are 'indefinite entities' (they arise from the interpretation of indefinite noun phrases) or both are not, it suffices to share all information about similarly-named dependencies ('match'). Otherwise, it is necessary to investigate whether dependencies should be copied from the definite to the indefinite entity ('copy'). The dependency lists are retrieved by the predicate 'deplist'. This also returns as the fourth argument the 'simplest' world model token that is known to correspond to the same object in the world. The predicate 'dep', which looks at the internal structure of a dependency, is discussed in Section V.10.1. Finally, 'distrib' calls 'generate', which invokes the specified semantic operation for each subcase.

```
distrib(E1,E2,K,F,X) :-
   indef(E1), indef(E2), !,
   deplist(E1,X,L1,_),
   deplist(E2,X,L2,_),
   match(L1,L2),
   generate(E1,L1,E2,L2,_,K,F,X).
distrib(E1,E2,K,F,X) :-
   indef(E1), !,
   deplist(E1,X,L1,_),
   deplist(E2,X,L2,E3),
   copy(L2,L1),
   generate(E1,L1,E3,L2,_,K,F,X).
distrib(E1,E2,K,F,X) :-
   indef(E2), !,
   deplist(E1,X,L1,E3),
   deplist(E2,X,L2,_),
   copy(L1,L2),
   generate(E3,L1,E2,L2,_,K,F,X).
distrib(E1,E2,K,F,X) :-
   deplist(E1,X,L1,E3),
   deplist(E2,X,L2,E4),
   match(L1,L2),
   generate(E3,L1,E4,L2,_,K,F,X).

copy(L,_) :- empty(L), !.
copy(L1,L2) :- list(L1,D,R), dmakein(D,L2), copy(R,L2).

    dmakein(D,L) :- empty(L), dep(D,external,_,_,_,_), !.
    dmakein(D,L) :- empty(L), !,
         dep(D,Na,_,_,Nu,Us), dep(D1,Na,_,_,Nu,Us), L = [D1 | _].
    dmakein(D,L) :- list(L,D1,L1),
         (dmatches(D,D1); makein(D,L1)), !.

match(L,_) :- empty(L), !.
match(L1,L2) :- list(L1,D,R),
    dtry(D,L2), match(R,L2).

    dtry(_,L) :- empty(L), !.
    dtry(D,L) :- list(L,D1,L1),
       (dmatches(D,D1); dtry(D,L1)), !.

    dmatches(D1,D2) :-
         dep(D1,Na,_,_,Nu,Us), dep(D2,Na,_,_,Nu,Us).
indef(E) :- atom(E).
list([A | B],A,B).
```

Fig. V.7 – First stage of semantic preprocessing

```
generate(E1,L1,E2,Env,Key,F,X) :- empty(L1), !,
    generate1(E1,E2,L2,Env,Key,F,X).
generate(E1,L1,E2,L2,Env,Key,F,X) :- list(L1,Dep,Rest),
    dep(Dep,Name,_,Type,Num,Use),
    (  var(Use)
        -> (enveval(Name,Env,Subs),
              generate(E1.Subs,Rest,E2,L2,Env,Key,F,X))
         ; gen(Num,Type,Name,E1,Rest,E2,L2,Env,Key,F,X)
    ).

    gen( 0,_,_,_,_,_,_,_,_,_,_).
    gen(N,Type,Name,E1,NewL1,E2,L2,Env,Key,F,X) :- N>0,
        nth(N,Type,E1,NewE1),
        enveval(Name,Env,N),
        generate(NewE1,NewL1,E2,Env,Key,F,X),
        N1 is N-1,
        gen(N1,Type,Name,E1,NewL1,E2,L2,Env,Key,F,X).

generate1(NewE1,E2,L2,_,Key,F,X) :- empty(L2), !,
    do(NewE1,E2,Key,F,X).
generate1(NewE1,E2,L2,Env,Key,F,X) :- list(L2,Dep,Rest),
    dep(Dep,Name,_,Type,Num,Use),
        (  envin(Name,Subs,Env)
        -> (nth(Subs,Type,E2,NewE2),
               generate1(NewE1,NewE2,Rest,Env,Key,F,X))
         ; ( var(Use) -> generate1(NewE1,E2._,Rest,Env,Key,F,X)
                      ; gen1(Num,Type,Name,NewE1,E2,Rest,Env,Key,F,X)
            )
        ).

    gen1( 0,_,_,_,_,_,_,_,_,_,_).
    gen1(N,Type,Name,NewE1,E2,NewL2,Env,Key,F,X) :- N>0,
        nth(N,Type,E2,NewE2),
        generate1(NewE1,NewE2,NewL2,Env,Key,F,X),
        N1 is N-1,
        gen1(N1,Type,Name,NewE1,E2,NewL2,Key,F,X).

    nth(N,subscr,E,E.N).
    nth(N,List,E,NewE) :- member(N,List,NewE).

    empty(X) :- var(X).
    list([A | B],A,B).

do(E1,E2,Key,F,X) :- Key =. .[Z | Args].
    append(Args,[E1,E2,F,X],NewArgs),
    Goal =. . [Z | NewArgs], call(Goal).
```

Fig. V.8 – Second stage of semantic preprocessing

The basic idea of 'generate' is to go through each of the dependency lists (L1 and L2) of the two entities involved (E1 and E2), adding 'subscripts' in all possible ways. A subscript converts the name of the typical element of a set to the name of a single element. Thus if 'particle1' is a typical element, then the elements are given by 'particle1.1', 'particle1.2', etc. obtained by adding the subscripts 1, 2, etc. While this is going on, an environment (Env) keeps track of what numbers are associated with which dependencies (dependencies with the same names must always be given the same subscripts). If a dependency is marked 'unused' (the component Use is a variable), it is not necessary (it may not even be possible) to generate numerical subscripts, and so a variable must be given as the subscript. Otherwise, all possible numbers up to the given maximum (Num) must be generated as subscripts. The generation of subscripts is, in fact, only relevant for certain dependencies. Sometimes a dependency will specify that the tokens standing for the set of objects are to be taken from a list. The 'nth' predicate decides according to the 'Type' of the dependency which of these is appropriate. Note that dependency lists are terminated by uninstantiated variables—hence the rather strange definition of 'empty'.

V.8   Semantic Operations

Figure V.9 gives some examples of routines implementing semantic operations. These are only invoked through the semantic preprocessors, and so it is not necessary to worry about sets of objects at this stage.

It is in the semantic operations that the actual assertions forming the program's output are generated. Some assertions generated are new information to be added to the database (predicate 'add'), some are constraints ('semantic checks') that must be satisfied (predicate 'test'), and some can

```
makeadj(light,O,F,X)  :- adddim(mass,[0,arbs],O,F,X).
makeadj(fixed,O,F,X) :- declare(F,fixed(O),X).

makenoun(C,G,F,X) :- ideal(C,I),
    declare(F,[isa(I,G)hasname(C,G)],X).

breakdown(M,[N,U],test,X) :- test(measure(M,N,U),X).
breakdown(M,[N,U],add,X) :-
    test(not(measure(M,*,*)),X),
    add(measure(M,N,U),X).

in(S,O,F,X) :-
    test(tsatisfies(container,O),X),
    declare(F,contains(O,S),X).

makecontact(O1,O2,F,X) :-
    test(separable(O1,O2),X),
    findpoints(O1,P1,F,X),
    findpoints(O2,P2,F,X),
    distrib(P1,P2,findcontact,F,X).
```

Fig. V.9 – Semantic operations

```
declare(add,L,X)  :- add(L,X).
declare(test,L,X) :- test(L,X).

add([ ],X) :- !.
add([L | Ls],X) :- !, conceal(L,X), add(Ls,X).
add(L,X) :- conceal(L,X).

test([ ],X) :- !.
test([L | Ls],X) :- !, test1(L,X), test(Ls,X).
test(L,X) :- test1(L,X).

   test1(L,X) :-
      functor(L,F,N), functor(L1,F,N),
      refsof(N,L,L1,X,R),
      incorp(R,L1,X).

   incorp(R,L,X) :- empty(R), !, deduce(L,X).
   incorp(R,L,X) :- list(R,_,Rest), empty(Rest),
      applyconstr(L,R,X,_).
   incorp(R,L,X) :- putin(R,L,R,X),
      applyconstr(L,R,X,_).
```

Fig. V.10 – Basic 'add' and 'test' operations

be either of these, according to the environment flag (predicate 'declare').
The top level of the code for these basic 'add' and 'test' operations is shown
in Fig. V.10.
Both 'add' and 'test' are designed to deal with either lists of assertions or
single assertions. 'add' simply involves storing the information in the
'clause datastructure' ('conceal'), where it can be found later by the inference system. 'test' involves first of all finding which unevaluated references
appear in the constraint using predicate 'refsof'. This returns the list of
them as its last argument and also rewrites the assertion to be expressed in
terms of their 'dedicated variables'—giving the 3rd argument. If there are
no unevaluated references, then satisfying the constraint simply involves
trying to 'deduce' the proposition. If there is more than one of them, it is
necessary to store the constraint for future use ('putin'). In any case where
there is at least one unevaluated reference, a non-trivial constraint satisfaction process ('applyconstr') must take place.
    The routine for dealing with inference ('deduce') is illustrated in
Fig. V.11.
    In order to deduce an assertion 'L', the system tries to find an assertion
that is the same or more general. (For instance, if the assertion is about an
element of a set, it might be necessary to establish that it is true for the
typical element.) For each argument of the assertion, the predicate 'up1' is
called to generate a name that is the same as or encompasses the one in
that position. Finally (when the first argument to 'up' is zero) an attempt is

```
    deduce(L,X) :- functor(L,F,N), functor(L1,F,N), up(N,L,L1,X).

    up(0,L,L1,X) :-
        (    discover(L1,X);
             clause(L1,true);
             (clause(L1,B), diff(B,true), deduceall(B,X))
        ),
        down(L1,X,L).
    up(N,L,L1,X) :- N>0,
        arg(N,L,A), arg(N,L1,B),
        up1(A,B,X),
        N1 is N−1, up(N1,L,L1,X).

    deduceall((G1,G2),X) :- !, deduceall(G1,X), deduceall(G2,X).
    deduceall((G1;G2),X) :- !, deduceall(G1,X); deduceall(G2,X).
    deduceall(G,X) ;- deduce(G,X).
```

Fig. V.11 – Inference

made to prove the assertion obtained. The first option is to find the assertion already stored explicitly ('discover' is the dual of 'conceal'). The next best thing is to find an inference rule that might enable it to be proved (using predicate 'clause'). If the rule has no antecedents ('clause(L1,true)'), we have succeeded; otherwise the antecedents will be the next things to prove.

V.9   The Clause Datastructure

The datastructure associated with a clause (the value of 'X' in most of the code) is represented as a Prolog term with functor 'sent' and arity 6. The 6 fields of the structure can be accessed via the following predicates:

1. roles(X,R)—R is the 'list' of syntactic roles filled. The list is terminated by a variable (rather than 'nil') so that new entries can easily be added. Each element of the list consists of the name of the role, the value that fills it and a variable that will become instantiated if the role is 'closed'.
2. modality(X,M)—M is the modality information about the proposition expressed by the clause (active/passive, past/present/future, etc.). This information is accessed, for instance, by the predicate 'ismood', which determines whether the clause is active or passive.
3. data(X,D)—D is the 'data area' for the clause. In fact, there is only really one data area, which is shared by all clause datastructures. This area includes the current database, the extra level of information about objects in the world model and information about which objects have been mentioned (for generating candidates for pronoun referents). For practical, rather than theoretical, reasons, the current database is

rewritten into its simplest form and transferred to the permanent Prolog database at the end of the processing of each input sentence.

4. per(X,P)—P is the symbol representing the time period at which the events described in the clause are interpreted as taking place. Because the program has no proper treatment of time, this symbol is always the same.

5. index(X,I)—this predicate is no longer used.

6. ident(X,I)—I is a structure containing information about the identity of the clause. This includes the name (used only for debugging purposes), the name of the previous clause and the 'level' (an integer which records how deeply embedded the clause is).

V.10   Representation of Objects

The following conventions are used for representing objects referred to by noun phrases. Objects introduced by indefinite noun phrases (in 'new' environments) are represented by Prolog atoms. Where a referent is known to be one of a set of candidates, a term of the form 'ref(N)' is used, where 'N' is an integer different from any one used previously in such a context. Where the referent is a set whose elements are provided by a given list, a term 'set(N)' is used, where 'N' is as before. The following paragraphs summarise the extra level of information kept about each kind of object. In addition to this, each object name is associated with every name that corresponds to the same object in the world by appearing in a tree representing this 'equivalence class'.

V.10.1   Indefinite Noun Phrases

The referent of an indefinite NP is represented as a Prolog atom. Associated with this (and kept in the 'data area' of the clause datastructure) is a dependency list, which says whether the atom stands for a single object or the typical element of a set. A dependency list is a list ending with a variable, because new entries will in general be created at various times througout the analysis. The components of each entry can be accessed through the predicate 'dep'—if 'Dep' is a 'dependency' then

dep(Dep,Name,_,Type,Num,Use)

means that

— 'Name' is the name of the dependency (giving some indication as to its origin),
— 'Type' (either 'subscr' or a list of object names) indicates how object names for the elements of the set are to be generated. 'subscr' specifies that the names can be derived by adding 'subscripts' (for instance, if the atom is 'particle1' and the only dependency specifies 'subscr' then the names are 'particle1.1', 'particle1.2', etc.). If instead the dependency specifies a list of names, then these are the names of the set elements,

— 'Num' specifies how many objects are in the set described by the dependency. It may be an integer, or an uninstantiated variable, if the number is not known,

— 'Use' specifies whether the division is into elements that are currently indistinguishable. An uninstantiated variable here means that there is currently no information in the database that enables the elements to be distinguished. If this is the case, the functioning of most semantic operations can consider the typical element without investigating the individual elements.

Where the code accesses dependencies by pattern-matching, rather than by using 'dep', the actual form of a dependency can be seen. In fact, it is represented by a term with functor 'dep' and arity 5, the arguments being in the same order as all but the first argument of the predicate 'dep'.

V.10.2   Singular Definite Noun Phrases
In general, the referent of a singular definite noun phrase is known to be the same as an object previously encountered, but it is not always known immediately which. The program represents the referent by a term 'ref(N)' and keeps extra information about what this is, as follows:

— A candidate list. This gives the names of the objects that it could correspond to. The candidate list is formed when the first constraint ('test') is made on the value, and gradually gets shorter as further constraints narrow down the possibilities. In fact, the list consists of terms of the form 'p(C,F)', where 'C' is the candidate and 'F' its current status (either 'in' or 'out', or an uninstantiated variable if it is not known whether it is the correct candidate or not).

— A list of constraints. These are constraints that link possible values with possible values of other unevaluated references. They are simple assertions with each occurrence of 'ref(N)', for some N, replaced by an occurrence of the dedicated variable of that reference (a Prolog variable). The list ends with a variable, so that new constraints can be added dynamically.

— A dedicated variable. This is used to stand for the reference in constraints that are being manipulated by the constraint satisfaction code. It becomes instantiated with the 'value' of the referent when that is known (if it is a single object).

— A list of the other unevaluated references that are mentioned in the stored constraints.

— A number. This gives the information about how many of the candidates are expected to be valid (1 for a singular noun phrase).

V.10.3   Plural Definite Noun Phrases
These referents are normally represented by terms of the form 'set(N)'. Associated with each such term is the list of elements of the set. The referent of a phrase starting with the word 'each' is represented by a term

'#X', where '#' is a defined prefix operator and 'X' is the term that would represent the corresponding plural definite noun phrase referent.

V.10.4   Getting Hold of Dependency Lists

Now that these details have been presented, some of the code for the predicate 'deplist' (as used in 'distrib') can be presented (Fig. V.12).

```
deplist(#E,X,[dep(E1,_,Type,Num,Use) | L],E1) :-
    deplist(E,X,[dep(external,_,Type,Num,Use) | L],E1).
deplist(set(N),X,[dep(external,_,L,Num,used) | _],N) :-
    findset(N,X,L), length(L,Num).
deplist(ref(N),X,L,E) :- findref(N,X,Cands,_,Var,_),
    refdeps(N,X,Cands,Var,L,E).
deplist(E,X,L,E) :- subz(E,X,L).
deplist([A],X,_,A).
deplist(L,X,[dep(external,_,L,Num,used) | _],[]) :- length(L,Num).

    refdeps(_,X,_,Var,L,E) :-
        nonvar(Var), !, deplist(Var,X,L,E).
    refdeps(N,X,Cands,_,_,ref(N)) :-
        allsimple(Ca,X), !.
    refdeps(N,X,_,_,L,E) :-
        instantiate(ref(N),X,V),
        deplist(V,X,L,E).

    subz(E.S,X,L) :- !, subz(E,X,[_ | L]).
    subz(E,X,L) :- atom(E), findindef(E,X,_,_,_,L).
```

Fig. V.12 – Getting hold of dependency lists

The first clause deals with the 'each' phrases—here, the dependency list differs only marginally from that of the corresponding plural phrase. The next case (for 'set(N)') just involves creating a dependency corresponding to the known list of elements (retrieved through 'findset'). For the case of 'ref(N)', there is an empty dependency list if all the candidates have empty dependency lists. Otherwise, a candidate is chosen ('instantiate'), and its dependency list is taken. The fourth clause deals with objects arising from indefinite noun phrases (possibly bearing 'subscripts'), and the last two cover lists of modifiers.

Appendix VI

PROGRAM TRACES

The following are some examples of traces produced by the computer program, exactly as they appear on the terminal. Some preliminary comments are necessary to explain the layout of the traces.

The program is written in a version of Prolog [Clocksin and Mellish 81] an interactive logic programming language. At the top level of the Prolog interpreter, the system displays the prompt ' | ?–' and reads a command from the user (terminated by a full stop). The command is then executed, the message 'yes' is displayed (assuming successful execution) and the system asks for another command.

The main commands for running the program are 'start', 'continue' and 'finish'. 'start' causes a sentence to be interpreted in a completely new context, whereas 'continue' is used for processing a sentence that follows on from previous input. 'finish' is used to carry out various housekeeping actions at the end of a mechanics problem. Not all the examples go through all these stages. Both 'start' and 'continue' causes a sentence to be read from the terminal (after the prompt ' | :'). This sentence is then processed by the program, with lines periodically being printed out to indicate its progress. At the end, the user is asked whether the 'new' information generated should be added to a permanent database for use in the analysis of further sentences. The program also displays the assertions on the terminal, expanding them out as necessary to express them completely in terms of 'unbroken' entities and no reference entities.

It is possible to alter the program so that it does not print out a fully exhaustive trace every time. The examples were run with different degrees of tracing, according to the degree of detail appropriate to them. Trace messages are basically of four kinds:

(starting with *)   Outline of clause level syntactic analysis
(starting with +)   Record of 'new' information generated
(starting with –)   Record of 'given' information generated
(starting with :)   Miscellaneous (e.g. filtering details)

These kinds are associated with decreasing priorities, so that every trace with ':' messages has all other kinds, every trace with '–' messages also has '+' and '*' messages, and so on. Sometimes, for reasons of space and clarity, parts of the traces are omitted. These are marked clearly with inserts such as

[. . .interpretation of noun phrases. . .]

The command 'what(X)' causes information about the entity with name 'X' to be displayed on the terminal.

Finally, it should be mentioned that integers preceded by the underline character, such as '_3397', are Prolog uninstantiated variables. The program also uses '*' as a way of denoting a variable for the special inference system.

VI.1 A Very Simple Example

This example illustrates the program working in the simple situation where all noun phrases introduce new objects and there is no mention of sets (this situation is described at the end of Chapter 2). Following the '*' lines, one can see that the program identifies three main constituents at the clause level of this example—the subject, main verb group and the prepositional phrase—before coming to the final punctuation. The noun phrases that are the subject of the sentence and the object to the preposition ('prepobject') are represented in the form 'A:B', where 'A' is a crude type ('physobj'—physical object) which is ascertained syntactically and 'B' is the name of the entity that arises from the interpretation of the phrase. Both phrases are interpreted as they are read, with 'new' (+) assertions generated to express the information conveyed and 'given' (–) assertions being satisfied as 'semantic checks'. The program displays a summary of the syntactic structure of the sentence before invoking the verb semantics.

| ?– start.

| : A particle of mass b rests on a smooth table.

+ new assertion isa(period,period1) recorded
* starting sentence1
* looking for subject
+ new assertion isa(particle,particle1) recorded
+ new assertion hasname(particle,particle1) recorded
– testing assertion thasprop(particle1,mass)
– test thasprop(particle1,mass) successful

+ new assertion mass(particle1,mass1,period1) recorded
- testing assertion not(measure(mass1,*,*))
- test not(measure(mass1,*,*)) successful
+ new assertion measure(mass1,b,arbs) recorded
* constituent physobj:particle1 found
* looking for mainverb
* constituent verbgr:mainverb(rest,[sing,actv,pres,inst]) found
* parsing prepositional phrase
+ new assertion isa(surface,table1) recorded
+ new assertion hasname(table,table1) recorded
- testing assertion thasprop(table1,coeff)
- test thasprop(table1,coeff) successful
+ new assertion coeff(table1,coeff1,period1) recorded
- testing assertion not(measure(coeff1,*,*))
- test not(measure(coeff1,*,*)) successful
+ new assertion measure(coeff1,0,arbs) recorded
* constituent prepobject:physobj:table1 found
* constituent binder: . found

* final parse of sentence1 following from start

* modality [sing,actv,pres,inst]
* roles filled
subject physobj:particle1
mainverb rest
pp pp(on,physobj:table1)

+ invoking rest semantics
+ invoking on semantics
- testing assertion not(tshape(table1,point))
- test not(tshape(table1,point)) successful
+ new assertion point_of(table1,point1) recorded
+ new assertion contact(particle1,point1,period1) recorded

* producing final assertions
add to database? n
measure(mass1,b,arbs)
measure(coeff1,0,arbs)
coeff(table1,coeff1,period1)
mass(particle1,mass1,period1)
contact(particle1,point1,period1)
isa(period,period1)
isa(particle,particle1)
hasname(particle,particle1)
isa(surface,table1)
hasname(table,table1)
point_of(table1,point1)

yes

VI.2   Examples with Definite Reference

The next two examples illustrate the creation and treatment of reference
entities. The first one does not present any special reference evaluation
problems, but shows how candidate sets are filtered and also illustrates the
symmetry in the handling of 'given' and 'new' environments. Thus the
referent of 'the pulley of weight 8 lbs' is gradually pinned down through
constraints on it and its weight. Also the semantics of 'hang' are used in a
'new' environment in the second sentence and in a 'given' environment in
the third. This example shows constraints being imposed which are really
'questions'—in the analysis of 'passing over' it is necessary to find an
appropriate central point on the string (tctrgravity(string1,_8438)).

The second example is to illustrate how the propagation of constraints
can help in reference evaluation. It is described more fully in Section 3.5.

Unfortunately, both of these examples have full tracing on to illuminate
some of the inner details. This means that there is a large volume of output.
One fact that may help to clarify the trace is that all semantic processing of
relative clauses takes place before the analysis of the head noun phrase is
complete. Hence the structure of embedded sentences is displayed by the
program before that of the main clauses.

| ?– start.

| : Two pulleys of weights 12 lb and 8 lb are connected by a
| : string passing over a fixed pulley .

+ new assertion isa(period,period1) recorded
* starting sentence1
* looking for subject
+ new assertion isa(pulley,pulley1) recorded
+ new assertion hasname(pulley,pulley1) recorded
– testing assertion thasprop(pulley1.2,weight)
– test thasprop(pulley1.2,weight) successful
+ new assertion weight(pulley1.2,weight1,period1) recorded
– testing assertion not(measure(weight1,*,*))
– test not(measure(weight1,*,*)) successful
+ new assertion measure(weight1,8,lbs) recorded
– testing assertion thasprop(pulley1.1,weight)
– test thasprop(pulley1.1,weight) successful
+ new assertion weight(pulley1.1,weight2,period1) recorded
– testing assertion not(measure(weight2,*,*))
– test not(measure(weight2,*,*)) successful
+ new assertion measure(weight2,12,lbs) recorded
* constituent physobj:pulley1 found
* holding aux
* constituent aux:are found
* looking for mainverb
* constituent verbgr:mainverb(connect,[plur,passv,pres,inst]) found

* parsing prepositional phrase
+ new assertion isa(string,string1) recorded
+ new assertion hasname(string,string1) recorded
* doing embedded sentence
* starting sentence2
* parsing prepositional phrase
+ new assertion isa(pulley,pulley2) recorded
+ new assertion hasname(pulley,pulley2) recorded
+ new assertion fixed(pulley2) recorded
* constituent prepobject:physobj:pulley2 found
* constituent binder: . found

* final parse of sentence2 following from sentence1

* modality [sing,actv,pres,cing]
* roles filled
subject physobj:string1
mainverb pass
pp pp(over,physobj:pulley2)

+ invoking pass semantics
+ invoking over semantics
− testing assertion tsatisfies(lineseg,string1)
− test tsatisfies(lineseg,string1) successful
− testing assertion tshape(string1,point)
− testing assertion tctrgravity(string1,_8438)
: filtering reference 1
: candidate midpoint valid
: filtering for 1 over
− test tctrgravity(string1,ref(1)) successful
− testing assertion thaspart(string1,midpoint)
− test thaspart(string1,midpoint) successful
+ new assertion midpt(string1,midpoint1) recorded
− testing assertion tshape(pulley2,point)
− test tshape(pulley2,point) successful
+ new assertion contact(midpoint1,pulley2) recorded
+ new assertion contact(pulley2,midpoint1) recorded
[. . .trying to recognise standard pulley system. . .]
* constituent prepobject:physobj:string1 found
* constituent binder: . found

* final parse of sentence1 following from start

* modality [plur,passv,pres,inst]
* roles filled
subject physobj:pulley1
mainverb connect
pp pp(by,physobj:string1)

+ invoking connect semantics
− testing assertion thaspart(string1,lend)
− test thaspart(string1,lend) successful
+ new assertion end(string1,lend1,left) recorded
+ new assertion isa(end,lend1) recorded
− testing assertion thaspart(string1,rend)
− test thaspart(string1,rend) successful
+ new assertion end(string1,rend1,right) recorded
+ new assertion isa(end,rend1) recorded
[. . .testing that 'pulley1.2' and 'rend1' can be in contact. . .]
+ new assertion fixed_contact(pulley1.2,rend1,period1) recorded
+ new assertion fixed_contact(rend1,pulley1.2,period1) recorded
[. . .trying to recognise standard pulley system. . .]
[. . .testing that 'pulley1.1' and 'lend1' can be in contact. . .]
+ new assertion fixed_contact(pulley1.1,lend1,period1) recorded
+ new assertion fixed_contact(lend1,pulley1.1,period1) recorded
[. . .trying to recognise standard pulley system. . .]

* producing final assertions
add to database? y
weight(pulley1.2,weight1,period1)
weight(pulley1.1,weight2,period1)
fixed(pulley2)
measure(weight1,8,lbs)
measure(weight2,12,lbs)
fixed_contact(pulley1.2,rend1,period1)
fixed_contact(rend1,pulley1.2,period1)
fixed_contact(pulley1.1,lend1,period1)
fixed_contact(lend1,pulley1.1,period1)
contact(midpoint1,pulley2)
contact(pulley2,midpoint1)
isa(period,period1)
isa(pulley,pulley1.1)
isa(pulley,pulley1.2)
hasname(pulley,pulley1.1)
hasname(pulley,pulley1.2)
isa(string,string1)
hasname(string,string1)
isa(pulley,pulley2)
hasname(pulley,pulley2)
isa(end,lend1)
isa(end,rend1)
midpt(string1,midpoint1)
end(string1,lend1,left)
end(string1,rend1,right)
end(string1,rend1,right)

yes

| ?– continue.

| : Over the pulley of weight 8 lbs is hung another string .

* starting sentence3
* parsing prepositional phrase
– testing assertion hasname(pulley,_720)
: filtering reference 6
: candidate pulley2 valid
: candidate pulley1.2 valid
: candidate pulley1.1 valid
: filtering for 6 over
– test hasname(pulley,ref(6)) successful
– candidates for pulley selected
– testing assertion weight(ref(6),_2097,period1)
: filtering reference 6
: candidate pulley2 invalid
: candidate pulley1.2 valid
: candidate pulley1.1 valid
: filtering for 6 over
: filtering reference 7
: candidate weight2 valid
: candidate weight1 valid
: filtering for 7 over
: filtering reference 7
: candidate weight2 valid
: candidate weight1 valid
: filtering for 7 over
– test weight(ref(6),ref(7),period1) successful
– testing assertion measure(ref(7),8,lbs)
: filtering reference 7
: candidate weight2 invalid
: candidate weight1 valid
: filtering for 7 over
: filtering reference 6
: candidate pulley1.2 valid
: candidate pulley1.1 invalid
: filtering for 6 over
: filtering reference 7
: candidate weight1 valid
: filtering for 7 over
– test measure(ref(7),8,lbs) successful
* constituent prepobject:physobj:ref(6) found
[. . .identifying main verb "hang" and new object 'string2'. . .]

* final parse of sentence3 following from sentence1

* modality [sing,passv,pres,inst]

* roles filled
pp pp(over,physobj:ref(6))
mainverb hang
subject physobj:string2

+ invoking hang semantics
[. . .deciding that the midpoint is required. . .]
+ new assertion midpt(string2,midpoint2) recorded
− testing assertion tshape(ref(6),point)
 : filtering reference 6
 : candidate pulley1.1 valid
 : filtering for 6 over
− test tshape(ref(6),point) successful
+ new assertion contact(midpoint2,ref(6)) recorded
+ new assertion contact(ref(6),midpoint2) recorded
[. . .trying to recognise standard pulley system. . .]

* producing final assertions
add to database? y
contact(midpoint2,pulley1.2)
contact(pulley1.2,midpoint2)
isa(string,string2)
hasname(string,string2)
midpt(string2,midpoint2)

yes
| ?− continue.

| : What is the acceleration of the string which
| : hangs over the fixed pulley ?
* starting sentence4
* looking for np to hold
* constituent measpair:what found
* holding aux
* constituent aux:is found
* looking for subject
− testing assertion hasname(string,_1732)
 : filtering reference 9
 : candidate string2 valid
 : candidate string1 valid
 : filtering for 9 over
− test hasname(string,ref(9)) successful
− candidates for string selected
* doing embedded sentence
* starting sentence5
* subject is physobj:ref(9)
* looking for mainverb
* constituent vergbr:mainverb(hang,[sing,actv,pres,inst]) found

* parsing prepositional phrase
– testing assertion hasname(pulley,_2452)
: filtering reference 10
: candidate pulley2 valid
: candidate pulley1.2 valid
: candidate pulley1.1 valid
: filtering for 10 over
– test hasname(pulley,ref(10)) successful
– candidates for pulley selected
– testing assertion fixed(ref(10))
: filtering reference 10
: candidate pulley2 valid
: candidate pulley1.2 invalid
: candidate pulley1.1 invalid
: filtering for 10 over
– test fixed(ref(10)) successful
* constituent prepobject:physobj:ref(10) found
* constituent binder: ? found

* final parse of sentence5 following from sentence4

* modality [sing,actv,pres,inst]
* roles filled
mainverb hang
subject physobj:ref(9)
pp pp(over,physobj:ref(10))

– invoking hang semantics
[. . .checking that both candidates of 'ref(9)' are stringlike. . .]
[. . .establishing that midpoints are involved. . .]
– testing assertion midpt(ref(9),_3168)
: filtering reference 9
: candidate string2 valid
: candidate string1 valid
: filtering for 9 over
: filtering reference 12
: candidate midpoint2 valid
: candidate midpoint1 valid
: filtering for 12 over
– test midpt(ref(9),ref(12)) successful
[. . .testing that 'ref(10)', ie 'pulley2', is a point. . .]
– testing assertion contact(ref(12),ref(10))
: filtering reference 10
: candidate pulley2 valid
: filtering for 10 over
: filtering reference 12
: candidate midpoint2 invalid
: candidate midpoint1 valid

: filtering for 12 over
: filtering reference 9
: candidate string2 invalid
: candidate string1 valid
: filtering for 9 over
[. . . . . .]
: filtering reference 12
: candidate midpoint1 valid
: filtering for 12 over
: filtering reference 10
: candidate pulley2 valid
: filtering for 10 over
− test contact(ref(12),ref(10)) successful
− testing assertion contact(ref(10),ref(12))
: filtering reference 12
: candidate midpoint1 valid
: filtering for 12 over
: filtering reference 10
: candidate pulley2 valid
: filtering for 10 over
− test contact(ref(10),ref(12)) successful
[. . .creating acceleration 'acceleration1' for 'string1'. . .]
− testing assertion acceleration(ref(9),_800,period1)
: filtering reference 9
: candidate string1 valid
: filtering for 9 over
: filtering reference 13
: candidate acceleration1 valid
: filtering for 13 over
− test acceleration(ref(9),ref(13),period1) successful
* constituent defmeas:ref(13) found
* constituent binder: . found
* main verb is be

* final parse of sentence4 following from sentence3

* modality [sing,actv,pres,inst]
* roles filled
subject defmeas:ref(13)
mainverb be
object#1 measpair:what

+ invoking be semantics
* producing final assertions
add to database? y
acceleration(string1,acceleration1,period1)

yes
| ?− finish.

* equation solving information
given(weight1)
given(weight2)
sought(acceleration1)
end of paragraph

yes

| ?– start.

| : A uniform rod is supported by a string attached to its ends.

+ new assertion isa(period,period1) recorded
* starting sentence1
* looking for subject
+ new assertion isa(rod,rod1) recorded
+ new assertion hasname(rod,rod1) recorded
– testing assertion thasprop(rod1,mass)
– test thasprop(rod1,mass) successful
+ new assertion uniform(rod1) recorded
* constituent physobj:rod1 found
* holding aux
* constituent aux:is found
* looking for mainverb
* constituent verbgr:mainverb(support,[sing,passv,pres,inst]) found
* parsing prepositional phrase
+ new assertion isa(string,string1) recorded
+ new assertion hasname(string,string1) recorded
* doing embedded sentence
* starting sentence2
* parsing prepositional phrase
– testing assertion mentioned(_2851,sing)
 : filtering reference 1
 : candidate string1 valid
 : candidate rod1 valid
 : filtering for 1 over
– test mentioned(ref(1),sing) successful
– candidates for pronoun selected
[. . .creating left ends 'lend1' and 'lend2'. . .]
[. . .for 'string1' and 'rod1'. . .]
– testing assertion end(ref(1),_3035,left)
 : filtering reference 1
 : candidate string1 valid
 : candidate rod1 valid
 : filtering for 1 over
 : filtering reference 2
 : candidate lend2 valid
 : candidate lend1 valid
 : filtering for 2 over

− test end(ref(1),ref(2),left) successful
[. . .creating right ends 'rend1' and 'rend2'. . .]
[. . .for 'string1' and 'rod1'. . .]
− testing assertion end(ref(1),_3213,right)
: filtering reference 1
: candidate string1 valid
: candidate rod1 valid
: filtering for 1 over
: filtering reference 3
: candidate rend2 valid
: candidate rend1 valid
: filtering for 3 over
− test end(ref(1),ref(3),right) successful
[. . . . . .]
∗ constitutent prepobject:physobj:set(1) found
∗ constituent binder: . found

∗ final parse of sentence2 following from sentence1

∗ modality [sing,passv,pres,inst]
∗ roles filled
subject physobj:string1
mainverb attach
pp pp(to,physobj:set(1))

+ invoking attach semantics
− testing assertion separable(string1,ref(3))
: filtering reference 3
: candidate rend2 valid
: candidate rend1 invalid
: filtering for 3 over
: filtering reference 1
: candidate string1 invalid
: candidate rod1 valid
: filtering for 1 over
: filtering reference 2
: candidate lend2 valid
: candidate lend1 invalid
: filtering for 2 over
: filtering reference 1
: candidate rod1 valid
: filtering for 1 over
: filtering reference 3
: candidate rend2 valid
: filtering for 3 over
− test separable(string1,ref(3)) successful
[. . .making other successful tests about 'ref(3)'. . .]
+ new assertion fixed_contact(lend1,ref(3),period1) recorded

+ new assertion fixed_contact(ref(3),lend1,period1) recorded
[. . .trying to recognise standard pulley system. . .]
− testing assertion separable(string1,ref(2))
 : filtering reference 2
 : candidate lend2 valid
 : filtering for 2 over
− test separable(string1,ref(2)) successful
[. . .applying more tests to 'ref(2)' and 'rend1'. . .]
+ new assertion fixed_contact(rend1,ref(2),period1) recorded
+ new assertion fixed_contact(ref(2),rend1,period1) recorded
[. . .trying to recognise standard pulley system. . .]
* constituent prepobject:physobj:string1 found
* constituent binder: . found

* final parse of sentence1 following from start

* modality [sing,passv,pres,inst]
* roles filled
subject physobj:rod1
mainverb support
pp pp(by,physobj:string1)

+ invoking support semantics
+ new assertion supports(string1,rod1) recorded

* producing final assertions
add to database? n
uniform(rod1)
supports(string1,rod1)
fixed_contact(lend1,rend2,period1)
fixed_contact(rend2,lend1,period1)
fixed_contact(rend1,lend2,period1)
fixed_contact(lend2,rend1,period1)
isa(period,period1)
isa(rod,rod1)
hasname(rod,rod1)
isa(string,string1)
hasname(string,string1)
isa(end,lend1)
isa(end,lend2)
isa(end,rend1)
isa(end,rend2)
end(string1,lend1,left)
end(rod1,lend2,left)
end(string1,rend1,right)
end(rod1,rend2,right)

yes

VI.3   Operations on Sets

The next three traces illustrate the program carrying out operations on sets. Some of the sets referred to end up represented as 'broken' entities, whereas others remain 'unbroken'. The 'what' commands after each example enable the final states of the entities to be inspected. The third example shows an instance of cardinality information being propagated through an 'external pairing' operation ('block1' starts off with an unknown number, but is later assigned the number '2' through the pairing with the ends of 'rod1').

| ?– start.

| : Two particles are attached to the left end of a string.

+ new assertion isa(period,period1) recorded
* starting sentence1
* looking for subject
+ new assertion isa(particle,particle1) recorded
+ new assertion hasname(particle,particle1) recorded
* constituent physobj:particle1 found
* holding aux
* constituent aux:are found
* looking for mainverb
* constituent verbgr:mainverb(attach,[plur,passv,pres,inst]) found
* parsing prepositional phrase
+ new assertion isa(string,string1) recorded
+ new assertion hasname(string,string1) recorded
+ new assertion end(string1,lend1,left) recorded
+ new assertion isa(end,lend1) recorded
* constituent prepobject:physobj:lend1 found
* constituent binder: . found

* final parse of sentence1 following from start

modality
* roles filled
subject physobj:particle1
mainverb attach
pp pp(to,physobj:lend1)

+ invoking attach semantics
+ new assertion fixed_contact(particle1,lend1,period1) recorded
+ new assertion fixed_contact(lend1,particle1,period1) recorded

* producing final assertions
add to database? n
fixed_contact(particle1,lend1,period1)
fixed_contact(lend1,particle1,period1)
isa(period,period1)

isa(particle,particle1)
hasname(particle,particle1)
isa(string,string1)
hasname(string,string1)
isa(end,lend1)
end(string1,lend1,left)

yes
| ?– what(particle1).

particle1 –
        indefinite entity, with dependency list [(external,2,F). . .]

yes
| ?– what(string1).

string1 –
        indefinite entity, with dependency list [. . .]

yes

| ?– start.
| : Particles of mass b and c are attached to the ends of a rod .

+ new assertion isa(period,period1) recorded
* starting sentence1
* looking for subject
+ new assertion isa(particle,particle1) recorded
+ new assertion hasname(particle,particle1) recorded
+ new assertion mass(particle1.2,mass1,period1) recorded
+ new assertion measure(mass1,c,arbs) recorded
+ new assertion mass(particle1.1,mass2,period1) recorded
+ new assertion measure(mass2,b,arbs) recorded
* constituent physobj:particle1 found
* holding aux
* constituent aux:are found
* looking for mainverb
* constituent vergbr:mainverb(attach,[plur,passv,pres,inst]) found
* parsing prepositional phrase
+ new assertion isa(rod,rod1) recorded
+ new assertion end(rod1,lend1,left) recorded
+ new assertion isa(end,lend1) recorded
+ new assertion end(rod1,rend1,right) recorded
+ new assertion isa(end,rend1) recorded
* constituent prepobject:physobj:set(1) found
* constituent binder: . found

* final parse of sentence1 following from start

* modality [plur,passv,pres,inst]

* roles filled
subject physobj:particle1
mainverb attach
pp pp(to,physobj:set(1))

+ invoking attach semantics
+ new assertion fixed_contact(particle1.2,rend1,period1) recorded
+ new assertion fixed_contact(rend1,particle1.2,period1) recorded
+ new assertion fixed_contact(particle1.1,lend1,period1) recorded
+ new assertion fixed_contact(lend1,particle1.1,period1) recorded

* producing final assertions
add to database? n
measure(mass1,c,arbs)
measure(mass2,b,arbs)
fixed_contact(particle1.2,rend1,period1)
fixed_contact(rend1,particle1.2,period1)
fixed_contact(particle1.1,lend1,period1)
fixed_contact(lend1,particle1.1,period1)
mass(particle1.2,mass1,period1)
mass(particle1.1,mass2,period1)
isa(peiod,period1)
isa(particle,particle1.1)
isa(particle,particle1.2)
hasname(particle,particle1.1)
hasname(particle,particle1.2)
isa(rod,rod1)
hasname(rod,rod1)
isa(end,lend1)
isa(end,rend1)
end(rod1,lend1,left)
end(rod1,rend1,right)

yes
| ?– what(particle1).

particle1 –
        indefinite entity, with dependency list [(external,2,T). . .]

yes
| ?– what(set(1)).

set(1) –
        set entity, with dependency list [(external,2,T). . .]
        and elements lend1,rend1

yes
| ?– what(mass1).

mass1 –
        indefinite entity, with dependency list [. . .]

yes

| ?– start.

| : Blocks of mass m are attached at the ends of a light rod .

+ new assertion isa(period,period1) recorded
* starting sentence1
* looking for subject
+ new assertion isa(particle,block1) recorded
+ new assertion hasname(block,block1) recorded
+ new assertion mass(block1,mass1,period1) recorded
+ new assertion measure(mass1,m,arbs) recorded
* constituent physobj:block1 found
* holding aux
* constituent aux:are found
* looking for mainverb
* constituent verbgr:mainverb(attach,[plur,passv,pres,inst]) found
* parsing prepositional phrase
+ new assertion isa(rod,rod1) recorded
+ new assertion hasname(rod,rod1) recorded
+ new assertion mass(rod1,mass2,peiod1) recorded
+ new assertion measure(mass2,0,arbs) recorded
+ new assertion end(rod1,lend1,left) recorded
+ new assertion isa(end,lend1) recorded
+ new assertion end(rod1,rend1,right) recorded
+ new assertion isa(end,rend1) recorded
* constituent prepobject:physobj:set(1) found
* constituent binder: . found

* final parse of sentence1 following from start

* modality [plur,passv,pres,inst]
* roles filled
subject physobj:block1
mainverb attach
pp pp(at,physobj:set(1))

+ new assertion invoking attach semantics
+ new assertion fixed_contact(block1.2,rend1,period1) recorded
+ new assertion fixed_contact(rend1,block1.2,period1) recorded
+ new assertion fixed_contact(block1.1,lend1,period1) recorded
+ new assertion fixed_contact(lend1,block1.1,period1) recorded

* producing final assertions
add to database? n
measure(mass1.1,m,arbs)
measure(mass1.2,m,arbs)
measure(mass2,0,arbs)
fixed_contact(block1.2,rend1,period1)

fixed_contact(rend1,block1.2,period1)
fixed_contact(block1.1,lend1,period1)
fixed_contact(lend1,block1.1,period1)
mass(block1.1,mass1.1,period1)
mass(block1.2,mass1.2,period1)
mass(rod1,mass2,period1)
isa(period,period1)
isa(particle,block1.1)
isa(particle,block1.2)
hasname(block,block1.1)
hasname(block,block1.2)
isa(rod,rod1)
hasname(rod,rod1)
isa(end,lend1)
isa(end,rend1)
end(rod1,lend1,left)
end(rod1,rend1,right)

yes
| ?– what(block1).

block1 –
        indefinite entity, with dependency list [(external,2,T). . .]

yes
| ?– what(mass1).

mass1 –
        indefinite entity, with dependency list [(external,2,T). . .]

yes
| ?– what(set(1)).

set(1) –
        set entity, with dependency list [(external,2,T). . .]
        and elements {lend1,rend1}

yes

VI.4   Plural Definite Phrases

The next two examples show the two different treatments of plural definite
phrases. In the first one, the entity 'ball1' is unbroken, and so there are no
individual elements available to be candidates for members of 'the balls'.
Thus the definite phrase is represented as a reference entity, with 'ball1' as
the only candidate. In the second example, the entity 'ball1' has been
broken by its association with the modifier 'of mass 5 and 6 lbs'. Thus 'the
balls' is represented as a 'set' entity, with the individual balls as its members.

| ?– start.

| : A man holds some uniform balls .

+ new assertion isa(period,period1) recorded
* starting sentence1
* looking for subject
+ new assertion isa(particle,man1) recorded
+ new assertion hasname(man,man1) recorded
* constituent physobj:man1 found
* looking for mainverb
* constituent verbgr:mainverb(hold,[sing,actv,pres,inst]) found
* looking for object
+ new assertion isa(particle,ball1) recorded
+ new assertion hasname(ball,ball1) recorded
+ new assertion uniform(ball1) recorded
* constituent physobj:ball1 found
* constituent binder: . found

* final parse of sentence1 following from start

* modality [sing,actv,pres,inst]
* roles filled
subject physobj:man1
mainverb hold
object#1 physobj:ball1

+ invoking hold semantics
+ new assertion supports(man1,ball1) recorded
+ new assertion fixed_contact(man1,ball1,period1) recorded
+ new assertion fixed_contact(ball1,man1,period1) recorded

* producing final assertions
add to database? y
uniform(ball1)
supports(man1,ball1)
fixed_contact(man1,ball1,period1)
fixed_contact(ball1,man1,period1)
isa(period,period1)
isa(particle,man1)
hasname(man,man1)
isa(particle,ball1)
hasname(ball,ball1)

yes
| ?– what(ball1).

ball1 –
         indefinite entity, with dependency list [(external,_,F). . .]

yes
| ?– continue.

| : The balls weigh 5 lbs .

* starting sentence2
* looking for subject
* constituent physobj:ref(1) found
* looking for mainverb
* constituent verbgr:mainverb(weigh,[plur,actv,pres,inst]) found
* looking for object
* constituent measpair:[[5,lbs]] found
* constituent binder: . found

* final parse of sentence2 following from sentence1

* modality [plur,actv,pres,inst]
* roles filled
subject physobj:ref(1)
mainverb weigh
object#1 measpair:[[5,lbs]]

+ invoking weigh semantics
+ new assertion mass(ball1,mass1,period1) recorded
+ new assertion measure(ref(2),5,lbs) recorded

* producing final assertions
add to database? n
measure(mass1,5,lbs)
mass(ball1,mass1,period1)

yes
| ?– what(ref(1)).

ref(1) –
        reference entity, with candidates {ball1}

yes
| ?– what(ref(2)).

ref(2) –
        reference entity, with candidates {mass1}

yes
| ?– what(mass1).

mass1 –
        indefinite entity, with dependency list [(external,_,F). . .]

yes

| ?– start.

| : A table supports two balls of mass 5 and 6 lbs .

+ new assertion isa(period,period1) recorded
* starting sentence1
* looking for subject
+ new assertion isa(surface,table1) recorded
+ new assertion hasname(table,table1) recorded
* constituent physobj:table1 found
* looking for mainverb
* constituent verbgr:mainverb(support,[sing,actv,pres,inst]) found
* looking for object
+ new assertion isa(particle,ball1) recorded
+ new assertion hasname(ball,ball1) recorded
+ new assertion mass(ball1.2,mass1,period1) recorded
+ new assertion measure(mass1,6,lbs) recorded
+ new assertion mass(ball1.1,mass2,period1) recorded
+ new assertion measure(mass2,5,lbs) recorded
* constituent physobj:ball1 found
* constituent binder: . found

* final parse of sentence1 following from start

* modality [sing,actv,pres,inst]
* roles filled
subject physobj:table1
mainverb support
object#1 pysobj:ball1

+ invoking support semantics
+ new assertion supports(table1,ball1.2) recorded
+ new assertion supports(table1,ball1.1) recorded

* producing final assertions
add to database? y
supports(table1,ball1.2)
supports(table1,ball1.1)
measure(mass1,6,lbs)
measure(mass2,5,lbs)
mass(ball1.2,mass1,period1)
mass(ball1.1,mass2,period1)
isa(period,period1)
isa(surface,table1)
hasname(table,table1)
isa(particle,ball1.1)
isa(particle,ball1.2)
hasname(ball,ball1.1)
hasname(ball,ball1.2)

yes
| ?- what(ball1).

ball1 −
          indefinite entity, with dependency list [(external,2,T). . .]

yes
| ?− continue.

| : The balls are uniform .

* starting sentence2
* looking for subject
* constituent physobj:set(1) found
* holding aux
* constituent aux:are found
* main verb is be
* looking for object
* constituent adj:uniform found
* constituent binder: . found

* final parse of sentence2 following from sentence1

* modality [plur,actv,pres,inst]
* roles filled
subject physobj:set(1)
mainverb be
object#1 adj:uniform

+ invoking be semantics
+ new assertion uniform(ball1.1) recorded
+ new assertion uniform(ball1.2) recorded

* producing final assertions
add to database? n
uniform(ball1.1)
uniform(ball1.2)

yes
| ?− what(set(1)).

set(1) −
          set entity, with dependency list [(external,2,T). . .]
          and elements {ball1.2,ball1.1}

yes

VI.5   'Each' Phrases

The last few traces illustrate examples of the treatment of 'each' phrases.
The first two examples show 'each' phrases of the two types, with the
underlying set entities unbroken and broken respectively. In the second
one, an indefinite phrase that is affected by the presence of the 'each' is
completely interpreted before the 'each' is read. The last example shows a

complicated situation where there are plural noun phrases and 'each' phrases all interacting. As a result, the entity 'block1' ends up with two distinct dependencies.

| ?– start.

| : Two men are standing on a scaffold.

+ new assertion isa(period,period1) recorded
* starting sentence1
* looking for subject
+ new assertion isa(particle,man1) recorded
+ new assertion hasname(man,man1) recorded
* constituent physobj:man1 found
* holding aux
* constituent aux:are found
* looking for mainverb
* constituent verbgr:mainverb(stand,[plur,actv,pres,cing]) found
* parsing prepositional phrase
+ new assertion isa(rod,scaffold1) recorded
+ new assertion hasname(scaffold,scaffold1) recorded
+ new assertion slope(scaffold1,hor) recorded
+ new assertion concavity(scaffold1,stline) recorded
* constituent prepobject:physobj:scaffold1 found
* constituent binder: . found

* final parse of sentence1 following from start

* modality [plur,actv,pres,cing]
* roles filled
subject physobj:man1
mainverb stand
pp pp(on,physobj:scaffold1)

+ invoking stand semantics
+ invoking on semantics
+ new assertion point_of (scaffold1,point1) recorded
+ new assertion contact(man1,point1,period1) recorded

* producing final assertions
add to database? y
concavity(scaffold1,stline)
slope(scaffold1,hor)
contact(man1,point1,period1)
isa(period,period1)
isa(particle,man1)
hasname(man,man1)
isa(rod,scaffold1)
hasname(scaffold,scaffold1)
point_of(scaffold1,point1)

yes
| ?- what(man1)

man1 –
      indefinite entity, with dependency list [(external,2,F). . .]

yes
| ?- continue.

| : Each man supports a uniform pole .

* starting sentence2
* looking for subject
* constituent physobj: #ref(1) found
* looking for mainverb
* constituent verbgr:mainverb(support,[sing,actv,pres,inst]) found
* looking for object
+ new assertion isa(rod,pole1) recorded
+ new assertion hasname(pole,pole1) recorded
+ new assertion uniform(pole1) recorded
* constituent physobj:pole1 found
* constituent binder: . found

* final parse of sentence2 following from sentence1

* modality [sing,actv,pres,inst]
* roles filled
subject physobj: #ref(1)
mainverb support
object#1 physobj:pole1

+ invoking support semantics
+ new assertion supports(man1,pole1) recorded

* producing final assertions
add to database? n
uniform(pole1)
supports(man1,pole1)
isa(rod,pole1)
hasname(pole,pole1)

yes
| ?- what(man1).

man1 –
      indefinite entity, with dependency list [(external,2,F). . .]

yes
| ?- what(ref(1)).

ref(1) –
      reference entity, with candidates {man1}

yes
| ?– what(pole1).

pole1 –
    indefinite entity, with dependency list [(man1,2,F)...]

yes

| ?– start.

| : A bridge 60 ft long is supported by a pier at each end .

+ new assertion isa(period,period1) recorded
∗ starting sentence1
∗ looking for subject
+ new assertion isa(rod,bridge1) recorded
+ new assertion hasname(bridge,bridge1) recorded
− testing assertion thasprop(bridge1,length)
− test thasprop(bridge1,length) successful
+ new assertion length(bridge1,length1,period1) recorded
− testing assertion not(measure(length1,*,*))
− test not(measure(length1,*,*)) successful
+ new assertion measure(length1,60,ft) recorded
∗ constituent physobj:bridge1 found
∗ holding aux
∗ constituent aux:is found
∗ looking for mainverb
∗ constituent verbgr:mainverb(support,[sing,passv,pres,inst]) found
∗ parsing prepositional phrase
+ new assertion isa(particle,pier1) recorded
+ new assertion hasname(pier,pier1) recorded
− testing assertion mentioned(_7990,sing)
− test mentioned(ref(1),sing) successful
− candidates for pronoun selected
[...creating left end 'lend1' for 'bridge1'...]
− testing assertion end(ref(1),_3196,left)
− test end(ref(1),ref(2),left) successful
[...creating right end 'rend1' for 'bridge1'...]
− testing assertion end(ref(1),_2708,right)
− test end(ref(1),ref(3),right) successful
[......]
+ invoking at semantics
[...testing various constraints on 'pier1.2' and 'ref(3)'...]
+ new assertion fixed_contact(pier1.2,ref(3),period1) recorded
+ new assertion fixed_contact(ref(3),pier1.2,period1) recorded
[...testing various constraints on 'pier1.1' and 'ref(2)'...]
+ new assertion fixed_contact(pier1.1,ref(2),period1) recorded
+ new assertion fixed_contact(ref(2),pier1.1,period1) recorded
[......]

* constituent prepobject:physobj:pier1 found
* constituent binder: . found

* final parse of sentence1 following from start

* modality [sing,passv,pres,inst]
* roles filled
subject physobj:bridge1
mainverb support
pp pp(by,physobj:pier1)

+ invoking support semantics
+ new assertion supports(pier1.2,bridge1) recorded
+ new assertion supports(pier1.1,bridge1) recorded
* producing final assertions
add to database? n
supports(pier1.2,bridge1)
supports(pier1.1,bridge1)
length(bridge1,length1,period1)
measure(length1,60,ft)
fixed_contact(pier1.2,rend1,period1)
fixed_contact(rend1,pier1.2,period1)
fixed_contact(pier1.1,lend1,period1)
fixed_contact(lend1,pier1.1,period1)
isa(period,period1)
isa(rod,bridge1)
hasname(bridge,bridge1)
isa(particle,pier1.1)
isa(particle,pier1.2)
hasname(pier,pier1.1)
hasname(pier,pier1.2)
isa(end,lend1)
isa(end,rend1)
end(bridge1,lend1,left)
end(bridge1,rend1,right)

yes
| ?– what(bridge1).

bridge1 –
        indefinite entity, with dependency list [. . .]

yes
| ?– what(pier1).

pier1 –
        indefinite entity, with dependency list [(1,2,T). . .]

yes

| ?– start.

| : Two boxes each containing 3 blocks of mass a b and c are
| : attached to the hinges of a door .

+ new assertion isa(period,period1) recorded
* starting sentence1
* looking for subject
+ new assertion isa(container,box1) recorded
+ new assertion hasname(box,box1) recorded
* doing embedded sentence
* starting sentence2
* looking for object
+ new assertion isa(particle,block1) recorded
+ new assertion hasname(block,block1) recorded
+ new assertion mass(block1.3,mass1,period1) recorded
+ new assertion measure(mass1,c,arbs) recorded
+ new assertion mass(block1.2,mass2,period1) recorded
+ new assertion measure(mass2,b,arbs) recorded
+ new assertion mass(block1.1,mass3,period1) recorded
+ new assertion measure(mass3,a,arbs) recorded
* constituent physobj:block1 found
* object2 is physobj:block1 . looking for object1
* constituent binder:implicit.comma found

* final parse of sentence2 following from sentence1

* modality [sing,actv,pres,cing]
* roles filled
subject physobj: #box1
mainverb contain
object#1 physobj:block1

+ invoking contain semantics
+ invoking in semantics
+ new assertion contains(box1,block1.3) recorded
+ new assertion contains(box1,block1.2) recorded
+ new assertion contains(box1,block1.1) recorded
* constituent physobj:box1 found
* holding aux
* constituent aux:are found
* looking for mainverb
* constituent verbgr:mainverb(attach,[plur,passv,pres,inst]) found
* parsing prepositional phrase
+ new assertion isa(door,door1) recorded
+ new assertion hasname(door,door1) recorded
+ new assertion hinge(door1,uhinge1,up) recorded
+ new assertion isa(end,uhinge1) recorded
+ new assertion hinge(door1,lhinge1,down) recorded
+ new assertion isa(end,lhinge1) recorded

* constituent prepobject:physobj:set(1) found
* constituent binder: . found

* final parse of sentence1 following from start

* modality [plur,passv,pres,inst]
* roles filled
subject physobj:box1
mainverb attach
pp pp(to,physobj:set(1))

+ invoking attach semantics
+ new assertion fixed_contact(box1.2,lhinge1,period1) recorded
+ new assertion fixed_contact(lhinge1,box1.2,period1) recorded
+ new assertion fixed_contact(box1.1,uhinge1,period1) recorded
+ new assertion fixed_contact(uhinge1,box1.1,period1) recorded

* producing final assertions
add to database? n
measure(mass1.1,c,arbs)
measure(mass1.2,c,arbs)
measure(mass2.1,b,arbs)
measure(mass2.2,b,arbs)
measure(mass3.1,a,arbs)
measure(mass3.2,a,arbs)
hinge(door1,uhinge1,up)
hinge(door1,lhinge1,down)
fixed_contact(box1.2,lhinge1,period1)
fixed_contact(lhinge1,box1.2,period1)
fixed_contact(box1.1,uhinge1,period1)
fixed_contact(uhinge1,box1.1,period1)
mass(block1.3.1,mass1.1,period1)
mass(block1.3.2,mass1.2,period1)
mass(block1.2.1,mass2.1,period1)
mass(block1.2.2,mass2.2,period1)
mass(block1.1.1,mass3.1,period1)
mass(block1.1.2,mass3.2,period1)
isa(period,period1)
isa(container,box1.1)
isa(container,box1.2)
hasname(box,box1.1)
hasname(box,box1.2)
isa(particle,block1.1.1)
isa(particle,block1.1.2)
isa(particle,block1.2.1)
isa(particle,block1.2.2)
isa(particle,block1.3.1)
isa(particle,block1.3.2)

hasname(block,block1.1.1)
hasname(block,block1.1.2)
hasname(block,block1.2.1)
hasname(block,block1.2.2)
hasname(block,block1.3.1)
hasname(block,block1.3.2)
isa(door,door1)
hasname(door,door1)
isa(end,uhinge1)
isa(end,lhinge1)
contains(box1.1,block1.3.1)
contains(box1.2,block1.3.2)
contains(box1.1,block1.2.1)
contains(box1.2,block1.2.2)
contains(box1.1,block1.1.1)
contains(box1.2,block1.1.2)

yes
| ?– what(set(1)).

set(1) –
  set entity, with dependency list [(external,2,T). . .]
  and elements {uhinge1,lhinge1}

yes
| ?– what(box1).

box1 –
  indefinite entity, with dependency list [(external,2,T). . .]

yes
| ?– what(block1).

block1 –
  indefinite entity,
  with dependency list [(external,3,T),(box1,2,T). . .]

yes

Appendix VII

BIBLIOGRAPHY

[Allen 83] Allen, J. Recognizing Intentions from Natural Language Utterances. In Brady, M. and Berwick, R. C., editors, *Computational Models of Discourse*. MIT Press, 1983.

[Appelt 81] Appelt, D. E. *Planning Natural Language Utterances to Satisfy Multiple Goals*. PhD dissertation, Stanford University, 1981.

[Barwise and Perry 83] Barwise, J. and Perry, J. *Situations and Attitudes*. Bradford Books, 1983.

[Bobrow and Webber 80] Bobrow, R. and Webber, B. PSI–KLONE—Parsing and Semantic Interpretation in the BBN Natural Language Understanding System. In *Procs of the CSCSI/CSEIO Annual Conference*, 1980.

[Brady and Wielinga 77] Brady, J. M. and Wielinga, B. J. *Reading the Writing on the Wall*. Technical Report, Department of Computer Science, University of Essex, 1977.

[Brown and Burton 75] Brown, J. S. and Burton, R. R. Multiple Representations of Knowledge for Tutorial Reasoning. In Bobrow, D. C. and Collins, A., editors, *Representation and Understanding*. Academic Press, 1975.

[Bundy et al., 79] Bundy, A., Byrd, L., Luger, G., Mellish, C. and Palmer, M. Solving Mechanics Problems using Meta-Level Inference. In *Procs of the Sixth International Joint Conference on Artificial Intelligence*. IJCAI, 1979.

[Bundy et al., 82] Bundy, A., Byrd, L. and Mellish, C. Special Purpose, but Domain Independent, Inference Mechanisms. In *Procs. of the European Conference on Artificial Intelligence*, 1982.

[Burstall 69] Burstall, R. M. A Program for Solving Word Sum Puzzles. *Computer Journal* **12**:48–51, 1969.

[Chafe 76] Chafe, W. L. Givenness, Contrastiveness, Definiteness, Subjects, Topics, and Point of View. In Li, C. N., editor, *Subject and Topic*. Academic Press, 1976.

[Charniak 72] Charniak, E. *Towards a Model of Children's Story Comprehension*. PhD thesis, MIT AI Laboratory, 1972.

[Christaller and Metzing 83] Christaller, T. and Metzing, D. Parsing Interactions and a Multi-Level Parser Formalism based on Cascaded ATNs. In Sparck-Jones, K. and Wilks, Y., editors, *Automatic Natural Language Parsing*. Ellis Horwood, 1983.

[Clark and Gregory 81] Clark, K. L. and Gregory, S. *A Relational Programming Language for Parallel Programming*. Technical Report, Imperial College, 1981.

[Clark and Marshall 78] Clark, H. H. and Marshall, C. Reference Diaries. In *TINLAP-2: Theoretical Issues in Natural Language Processing*. Association for Computational Linguistics, New York, 1978

[Clocksin and Mellish 81] Clocksin, W. and Mellish, C. *Programming in Prolog*. Springer Verlag, 1981.

[Cohen 78] Cohen, P. *On Knowing What to Say: Planning Speech Acts*. Technical Report No. 118, University of Toronto, 1978.

[Colmerauer 77] Colmerauer, A. *An Interesting Subset of Natural Language*. Technical Report, Groupe d'Intelligence Artificielle, Universite d'Aix-Marseille, France, 1977.

[Cottrell and Small 83] Cottrell, G. W. and Small, S. L. A Connectionist Scheme for Modelling Word Sense Disambiguation. *Cognition and Brain Theory* **6**, 1983.

[Donnellan 71] Donnellan, K. Reference and Definite Descriptions. In Steinberg, D. and Jakobovits, L., editors, *Semantics*. Cambridge University Press, 1971.

[Doyle 79] Doyle, J. A Truth Maintenance System. *Artificial Intelligence* **12**, 1979.

[Dull, Metcalfe and Williams 64] Dull, C. E., Metcalfe, H. C. and Williams, J. E. *Modern Physics*. Holt, Rinehart and Winston, 1964.

[Freuder 78] Freuder, E. C. Synthesising Constraint Expressions. *Communications of the ACM* **21**:958–966, 1978.

[Frisch 85] Frisch, A. Parsing with Restricted Quantification. In *Proceedings of the AISB Conference, Warwick*, 1985.

[Grice 75] Grice, H. P. Logic and Conversation. In Cole, P. and Morgan, J., editors, *Syntax and Semantics*. Academic Press, 1975.

[Grossman 76] Grossman, R. W. *Some Data Base Applications of Constraint Expressions*. Technical Report 158, Laboratory for Computer Science, MIT, 1976.

[Grosz 77] Grosz, B. *The Representation and Use of Focus in Dialogue Understanding*. Technical Note 151, SRI Iternational, Menlo Park, California, 1977.

[Halliday 67] Halliday, M. A. K. Notes on Transitivity and Theme in English: II. *Journal of Linguistics* **3**:199, 1967.

[Haviland and Clark 74] Haviland, S. and Clark, H. What's new? Acquiring New Information as a Process in Comprehension. *Journal of Verbal Learning and Verbal Behaviour* **13**:512–521, 1974.

[Hinton and Anderson 81] Hinton, G. E. and Anderson, J. A. *Parallel Models of Associative Memory*. Lawrence Erlbaum Associates, 1981.

[Humphrey 57] Humphrey, D. *Intermediate Mechanics, Dynamics*. Longman, Green & Co, 1957.

[Johnson-Laird 83] Johnson-Laird, P. N. *Mental Models*. Cambridge University Press, 1983.

[Katz and Fodor 64] Katz, J. and Fodor, J. The Structure of a Semantic Theory. In Fodor, J. and Katz, J., editors, *The Structure of Language*. Prentice-Hall, 1964.

[Kay 1980] Kay, M. *Algorithm Schemata and Data Structures in Syntactic Processing*. Report CSL-80-12, Xerox PARC, 1980.

[Loney 39] Loney, S. L. *The Elements of Statics and Dynamics*. Cambridge University Press, 1939.

[Mackworth 77] Mackworth, A. Consistency in Networks of Relations. *Artificial Intelligence* **8**:99–118, 1977.

[Marcus 79] Marcus, M. *Overview of a Theory of Syntactic Recognition for Natural Language*. Technical Report TR-531, AI Lab, MIT, 1979.

[McKenzie 60] McKenzie, A. E. *A Second Course of Mechanics and Properties of Matter*. Cambridge University Press, 1960.

[Mellish 78] Mellish, C. S. *Preliminary Syntactic Analysis and Interpretation of Mechanics Problems Stated in English*. Working Paper 48, Dept of Artificial Intelligence, University of Edinburgh, 1978.

[Mellish 82] Mellish, C. S. *Incremental Evaluation: An Approach to the Semantic Interpretation of Noun Phrases*. Cognitive Studies Research Paper 001, University of Sussex, 1982.

[Mellish 83] Mellish, C. S. *Incremental Evaluation: an Approach to the Semantic Interpretation of Noun Phrases*. Research Paper CSRP 001, Cognitive Studies Programme, University of Sussex, 1983.

[Mellish 83a] Mellish, C. S. Incremental Semantic Interpretation in a Modular Parsing System. In Sparck-Jones, K. and Wilks, Y., editors, *Automatic Natural Language Parsing*. Ellis Horwood, 1983.

[Milne 83] Milne, R. *Resolving Lexical Ambiguity in a Deterministic Parser*. PhD thesis, University of Edinburgh, 1983.

[Novak 76] Novak, G. S. *Computer Understanding of Physics Problems Stated in Natural Language*. Technical Report NL-30, Computer Science Dept, University of Texas at Austin, 1976.

[Palmer 81] Palmer, M. *Driving Semantics in a Limited Domain*. PhD thesis, Dept of Artificial Intelligence, University of Edinburgh, 1981.

[Pereira and Warren 80] Pereira, F. C. N. and Warren, D. H. D. Definite Clause Grammars Compared with Augmented Transition Networks. *Artificial Intelligence* **13**(3), 1980.

[Richards *et al.*, 66] Richards, Sears, Wehr and Zemansky. *Modern University Physics*. Volume 1: *Mechanics and Thermodynamics*. Addison-Wesley, 1966.

[Riesbeck 75] Riesbeck, C. K. Computational Understanding. In Schank, R. and Nash-Webber, B. L., editors, *Theoretical Issues in Natural Language Processing*. Association of Computational Linguistics, 1975.

[Ritchie 76] Ritchie, G. D. Problems in Local Semantic Processing. In Brady, M., editor, *Proc of the AISB Conference, Edinburgh*. AISB, 1976.

[Ritchie 77] Ritchie, G. D. *Computer Modelling of English Grammar*. PhD thesis, Dept of Computer Science, University of Edinburgh, September 1977.

[Schank *et al.*, 75] Schank, R. C. and the Yale AI Project. *SAM—a Story Understander*. Research Report #43, Yale University Dept of Computer Science, 1975.

[Shadbolt 85] Shadbolt, N. Forthcoming PhD thesis, University of Edinburgh, 1985.

[Shapiro 83] Shapiro, E. Y. *A Subset of Concurrent Prolog and its Interpreter*. Technical Report, Weizmann Institute of Science, 1983.

[Sidner] Sidner, C. L. *Towards a Computational Theory of Definite Anaphora Comprehension in English Discourse*. PhD thesis, Dept of Electrical Engineering and Computer Science, MIT, 1979.

[Simmons 73] Simmons, R. F. Semantic Networks: Their Computation and Use for Understanding English Sentences. In Schank, R. C. and Colby, K. M., editors, *Computer Models of Thought and Language*. Freeman & Co, 1973.

[Street 29] Street, R. O. *Examples in Applied Mathematics*. Methuen, 1929.

[Vanlehn 78] Vanlehn, K. A. *Determining the Scope of English Quantifiers*. Technical Report TR-483, AI Lab, MIT, 1978.

[Waltz 72] Waltz, D. *Generating Semantic Descriptions from Drawings of Scenes with Shadows*. Technical Report, MIT, 1972.

[Waltz and Pollack 84] Waltz, D. L. and Pollack, J. B. *Massively Parallel Parsing: A Strongly Interactive Model of Natural Language Interpretation*. Working Paper 48, Coordinated Science Laboratory, University of Illinois, 1984.

[Webber 79] Webber, B. L. *A Formal Approach to Discourse Anaphora*. Garland Publishing Inc, New York, 1979.

[Wilks 75] Wilks, Y. A Preferential Pattern-seeking, Semantics for Natural Language Inference. *Artificial Intelligence* **6**:53–74, 1975.

[Winograd 72] Winograd, T. *Understanding Natural Language*. Academic Press, 1972.

[Winston 77] Winston, P. H. *Artificial Intelligence*. Addison Wesley, 1977.

[Woods *et al.*, 72] Woods, W. A. *et al. The Lunar Sciences Natural Language Information System: Final report*. Report No. 2378, BBN, 1972.

[Woods 75] Woods, W. A. What's in a Link: Foundations for Semantic

Networks. In Bobrow, D. and Collins, A., editors, *Representation and Understanding*. Academic Press, 1975.

[Woods 77] Woods, W. A. *Semantics and Quantification in Natural Language Question Answering*. Technical Report No. 3687, BBN, 1977.

[Woods 80] Woods, W. A. Cascaded ATN Grammars. *American Journal of Computational Linguistics* **6**, 1, 1980.

INDEX

abstractness, levels of in entities, 90–91,
  98–99, 101
ATN, 113
  cascaded, 114
arc consistency, 46–52, 57
attributive, 45

backtracking, 32, 45, 113 (see choices,
  search space)
'be' (as copula), 62
beliefs, 61, 116
Bobrow, R., 26, 34, 84
Brady, M., 26
broken, 66, 79, 91, 96–97
Brown, J., 21, 22
Burton, R., 21, 22

candidate set, 44, 76–80
cardinality, 24, 63, 89, 104, 108–109
Charniak, E., 21, 22, 56
chart, 114
  semantic, 114
choices
  in complex candidate sets, 80
  in early semantic analysis, 111
  in processing sets, 74, 94
  in semantic operations, 53
  in semantic preprocessing, 80
  in syntactic processing, 14, 18
  independence of, 55, 114
  introduced by reference rule, 98
Clark, H., 36, 116
coextension, 61–62, 97–99
Colmerauer, A., 24, 95
combinatoric aspects of semantic interpretation, 84
commands, 22, 107
compound entity rule, 99–101
computer vision, 26, 57
connectionist machines, 117
consistency
  node, 57
  arc, 46–52, 57
  path, 57
constraints
  complex, 106
  diagrammatic notation for, 48–49, 51

in natural language processing, 42
propagation of, 46–48
satisfaction of, 46–48, 57–59, 121–123
type, 117
context, 19, 20, 130
control annotations, 115
corresponding elements (see external pairing)

database, 32, 52
  queries to, 52, 97
datastructure, clause, 131–132,
  143–144
definite clause grammar (DCG), 32,
  132–137
definite noun phrases
  plural, 76–83
  plural, examples, 164–168
  proper, 18, 76–80
  reference examples, 150–159
demon, 56
dependency list, 64–66, 124–126
  format in program, 144–146
  notation for, 66
  of function value, 130
  restrictions of, 108–109
  summary of rules, 124–126
determinism, 113–114
distributive, 64, 78, 93–94
Donnellan, K., 45

'each', 80–82, 86–89, 105, 107
  examples, 168–174
early semantic analysis, 14, 110–111
end of noun phrase interpretation,
  18–21
entity in world model, 62, 67, 73
  representation of in program, 144–146
environment (given/new), 37, 129–130, 132,
  142
essential properties, 73–74
'evoke', 73
exhaustive descriptions, 78, 105
external
  decomposition, 64, 65
  pairing, 71, 84, 85

filtering, 46
finalisation of set references, 78–79
finiteness
    of candidate lists, 44, 116
    of sets, 31, 73, 108, 116
focus, 56
function, 106, 129–130

given information, 36, 42–43 (see constraints)
given/new, 36–37
    examples, 148–149
Grice, H., 50
Grosz, B., 22

Haviland, S., 36
history list, 22
hyperarc, 57

inconsistency, 116–117
incremental semantic interpretation, 26, 110, 115, 116–117
indefinite noun phrase, 22, 60–75
    plural, 63–64, 79
inference, 96–102, 142–143
    optimistic, 102
    pessimistic, 102
    rule, 99, 101
    rule, special, 96–102
intension, 62, 73
interpretation, levels of, 15–17, 111

Johnson-Laird, P., 115

Kay, M., 114

linking, 71, 85, 86, 88, 89, 92, 100
logic programming, 115

Mackworth, A., 57–58
Marcus, M., 26, 113–114
maximality assumption, 78, 105
mechanics problems, 30
model of world, 15, 115 (see entity)

negation, logical, 101–102
new information, 36
    about reference entities, 45, 97–99
    about sets, 77, 94
node consistency, 57
non-specific, 109
Novak, G., 18, 22, 23

operators, logical, 108

parallelism, 115
parsing (see syntactic processing)
plural phrases, 63–64, 76–80, 104–105, 105
possessives, 49
predicate, 127–128
prediction, 56–57
preference semantics, 56, 117

Prolog, 32, 147
pronouns, 21, 107

quantification, 24, 63, 80–82, 86–89, 105
    examples, 168–174
    indirect dependencies, 92–93, 106
quantifiers, 108
questions, 22, 107
'questions', 52

reference evaluation, 103–104
    role of beliefs in, 116
    rule, 97–99, 101
    to 'each' phrases, 107
    unevaluated, 43
referent, 11, 15
referential, 109
Reisbeck, C., 13
Ritchie, G., 19

Schank, R., 21, 22, 56
script, 56, 57
search space (see choices)
semantic
    check, 36, 42, 45, 107, 128
    marker, 16
    operation, 35, 38, 52–55, 84, 141–143
    preprocessor, 84–95, 125–126, 136–141
semantics, situation, 116
sets, 63–95, 104–105
    functions of, 130
    of sets, 106
    processing examples, 160–164
sharing of dependency information, 89
sub-entities (see subscripting)
subscripting, 67–69, 100
subsets, 108–109
syntactic
    ambiguity, 18
    constraints, 43
    processing, 32–33, 113–114, 132–135
    /semantic interface, 33–35, 114–115, 133–135
    structure, 12

TMS, 114
two-stage appraoch to semantic interpretation, 12
typical element, 63–64, 66–73, 100, 104

underspecified assertions, semantics of, 45, 66–73, 96–102
usage flag, 66, 100

Vanlehn, K., 106

Waltz, D., 57–59
Webber, B., 26, 34, 73, 81, 84, 107
Wilks, Y., 42, 56
Winograd, T., 18, 22
Woods, W., 21, 24, 95, 109, 114
world model (see entity)